Interior Gardens

A New York Memoir

KIM PARKER

Blossom Books

Contents

Interior Gardens   1

Dedication   3

Copyright   5

Prelude   6

1. Permission   9
2. Rite of Passage   12
3. An Insurance Company   16
4. High Fidelity   18
5. Musical Indignities   23
6. I'm sorry Mr. Netanyahu   28
7. Turning Point   31
8. The Children's Museum   34
9. A New Life in Belgium   36
10. Coming Home   41
11. A Kite Without A String   43
12. ECHO Chamber   46
13. Painting for a Living   51

14.	Benjamin Braddock at the Whitney	54
15.	Happy Halloween	60
16.	The Carriage House Series	64
17.	An Early Exhibit	66
18.	Farewell to 9 to 5	70
19.	Kim Parker Designs	72
20.	Intimate Exchange	77
21.	The King of the Fashion Industry	80
22.	"My Little Victoria's Secret"	84
23.	Meeting Liena	88
24.	A Striped Past	94
25.	It's a Wrap	99
26.	Jill loves Pink Too	102
27.	Wisdom in a Schmatta House	104
28.	A Spacious Loft in Herald Square	107
29.	Liz Claiborne and the Launch of a Brand	110
30.	The Writing on the Wallpaper	113
31.	No Elephants in the Garden	118
32.	Mums and Asters	124
33.	41 Madison Avenue and Spode	130
34.	James McEnearny	133
35.	Growing a Spine	136
36.	Harry N. Abrams	140

37.	A Visit From Jim Thompson	145
38.	A Bloomingdale's Launch	150
39.	Trade Shows and Horses	153
40.	Clinique	156
41.	Paul Poiret: The King Of Fashion	161
42.	Realization	166
43.	Mikasa	168
44.	Farewell to a New York Treasure	172
45.	The Psychic in Hell's Kitchen	175
46.	A Unique Manhattan Enclave	186
47.	"You Are The Flower Market"	189
48.	The Robin's Song	192
49.	Playing for Jean Pierre Rampal	194
50.	A Sabbatical at Oberlin	200
51.	The Last Flute Lesson	204
52.	Confirmations	206
53.	Taking Flight	208
54.	A Nod from the Universe	212
55.	Coming of Age on Seventh Avenue	214
56.	"Your Gardens Are Full Of Stories"	218
57.	Lizzie's Visit	223
58.	TJ	228
59.	Manifestation: A London Launch	232

60. Reflections in a Taxi	237
61. A Magic Flute	240
62. Vuillard House	244
63. Bernstein at Greenwood Cemetery	248
64. About the Author	251

Interior Gardens

A New York Memoir

"If you are going to fall off a ladder, fall off a high rung."

Leonard Bernstein

KIM PARKER

Dedication

I wish to dedicate this book to my dear family – my mother Carol, my father Guy, my brother Dennis and husband Felipe, for their unwavering support and love. I would also like to include my late "stepfather" Ernie, my Buddhist healer Gil, and my two furry dog daughters, Maggie and Wendy – for their love felt in spirit.

Copyright

Copyright © Kim Parker 2023. All rights reserved.

No part of this book may be reproduced, stored in a retrieval system, or transmitted in any form or by any means, electronic, mechanical, photocopying, recording, or otherwise, without the express written permission of the author or publisher. For permissions requests please email: info@kimparker.tv

Text copyright 2023 by Kim Parker. All textile designs and fine art images on the cover and interior of this book, copyright 2023 by Kim Parker. Book Cover: Lush Garden by Kim Parker Copyright Kim Parker 2004. All rights reserved. Photo credits: Leonard Bernstein photo copyright Guy Parker 2008. Various photos of Kim Parker and Felipe Porto copyright Kim Parker 2023. Photo of Mikasa dinnerware copyright Lifetime Brands 2015. Textile design images copyright Kim Parker 2023. Ariadne's Dream wallpaper interior photo credit copyright Clarke & Clarke UK 2015. Editor: Felipe Porto Graphic Design: Felipe Porto Production Manager: Felipe Porto

ISBN number: 979-8-218-17082-0 Library of Congress Cataloguing in Publication Data - Parker, Kim

Prelude

Painting gardens has always been a form of visual storytelling for me, and that's what has kept the process fresh. The gardens that became my signature style in the Art and Design industries, secretly held these stories in their choreography. Flowers and stems were the main characters, bending and leaping, some broken, others, exalted. The vivid colors represented my insatiable desire and inner yearning for love and harmony, with a dash of dissonance. For more than three decades of my New York City life, finding my way towards self expression and creative freedom, I became a bit of a Houdini, kicking free when something caged my spirit. And I've become well aware that what we visualize, we materialize, both good and bad. Every encounter, growing pain, lesson and triumph all had their place in the garden. I always held an inextinguishable vision in my heart and mind, and believed in its eventual manifestation.

It was a Nepalese older woman who visited my home one day, and who took me aside after carefully studying one of my garden paintings over the sofa, and said:

"Kim, I can see that your gardens are full of stories." My eyes filled with tears. She was right. There would always be stories.

Leonard Bernstein at Tanglewood

Permission

"Flute, what's your name?" Leonard Bernstein asked smiling a few feet away on the podium. "Kim," I replied softly. "We are going to start from the flute solo. Just follow my baton. I will conduct you through it and cue the strings when it is time for them to enter," he said gently.

I was sixteen at Tanglewood that summer, when Leonard Bernstein composed his *"Divertimento For Orchestra"* a centenary commission to be premiered by The Boston Symphony Orchestra. My flute teacher, Paul Fried, was the former Associate Principal Flutist of the BSO. "Kim," he said smiling, after posting the flute positions, "I have assigned you principal flute under Leonard Bernstein tomorrow morning in rehearsal. Your orchestra will be playing his new work, *"Divertimento."* We will be premiering the same piece tonight in the shed."

Leonard Bernstein had been my musical hero throughout my childhood; my bedroom bulletin board covered with his pictures, numerous articles saved from The NY Times and music publications. I used to secretly leap with joy to his New York Philharmonic recording of Beethoven's "Leonore Overture No. 3" behind my closed bedroom door.

"Paul," I said nervously, "Thank you so much for giving me the principal flute part but, how can I get a hold of the music before tomorrow morning's rehearsal?" "Don't worry, Kim," he said reassuringly, "I wouldn't have assigned you the part if I thought you couldn't handle it. Come to the concert tonight. After the concert is over, you can come backstage and get the music."

That evening I went to hear the BSO's premiere of "Divertimento." Throughout the premier of this new orchestral work, I listened intently, when suddenly, there was a lengthy flute solo, with no other instruments accompanying. From a distance it sounded beautiful and lyrical, but never having heard it before, I felt panicked to get my hands on the flute part as soon as possible.

After the concert was over I dashed backstage. I was told that the parts had already been collected and locked into the Tanglewood library for the night. This meant that I would not be able to see the music until the very next morning, with only a few minutes before rehearsal.

If we had been playing a Beethoven, Dvorak, Mahler or Tchaikovsky symphony any other orchestral work from the standard repertoire– I would not have felt nervous. I knew those flute parts well. However, playing Leonard Bernstein's music for Leonard Bernstein was altogether different. He was my musical hero.

The following morning, minutes before rehearsal, I opened the music and went directly to the solo flute passage. The meter changed every measure. I quickly looked over the passage while sitting alone in the grass.

Bernstein entered the rehearsal shed in clean white shirt and head of silky, silver hair. The string players tapped their bows upon their music stands and every member of the orchestra were stomping feet in applause upon his joyful entrance. "Good morning!" he said, exuberantly.

"And how many of you came to the concert last night to hear the BSO premiering my new work?" he asked curiously. Some of us raised our hands. Moments later, while thumbing through his score, he looked up, pointed his baton at me and with a smile asked, "Flute, what's your name?" Taking a quick breath and looking him directly in the eyes, I replied, "Kim." "We will start from the flute solo," he said. " The meter is a bit tricky. I will conduct you through it and I will cue the strings when it is time for them to enter."

For the first few measures I carefully watched Bernstein's every gesture following the tempo he had indicated. But after only a few bars, drawn into the lyrical beauty of his music, I played the solo as if I had known this music my entire life. One note led effortlessly to the next. I was no longer following his baton, but taking flight freely on my own. I was not even aware that Bernstein had stopped conducting, allowing me to continue playing the solo passage to the end.

When I finished, the Maestro stepped off the podium, parting his way through a Red Sea of music stands until he reached mine. He placed both hands on each side of my face, kissed me, and said, "My dear Kim, *you* are an artist."

When I look back at that summer at Tanglewood, I realize what an emotional milestone it was in my life. I knew that had I never performed again, I could go to my grave musically fulfilled. Over the years, I have come to understand the meaning of that moment with greater perspective and clarity. The Universe had not only given me the privilege of playing for my musical hero, but, even more Divinely, the gift of playing *his* music. That moment provided me with the greatest set of creative wings I could ever have asked for, freeing and permitting me to take artistic flight in *any* direction.

Rite of Passage

After many years of dedication to a career as a classical flutist with memorable summers in an orchestra at Tanglewood, performing in two consecutive Jean Pierre Rampal master classes by the age of fifteen, and graduating from Oberlin Conservatory of Music with a degree in Flute Performance, I decided to walk away from this promising, earlier career. My family, were all serious classical musicians. I had joined the family quartet at eight years old. Competitions, concerts and spending summers at Berkshire music festivals all seemed to point me in the direction of a career in music.

But after four years in Oberlin, Ohio, surrounded by cornfields, I longed for the energy and color of New York City life. By the end of college I was married to a man from Brazil. I didn't mind the idea of apartment life supported by some menial job that had nothing to do with my musical past. All I wanted at that time was to make a happy home for the two of us and pay our rent.

Domesticity and quietude was what I wanted at that time in my early twenties, and that is what I wound up with. My life moved swiftly from a high musical rung to the bottom of the corporate world in Manhattan. I was working in administrative positions that cared nothing for my musical past.

For a while I didn't mind the mundane aspect of my domestic life in Queens; boarding subway trains each morning and then sitting idly at reception desks for eight hours a day. It was my new reality. Like everyone, I had a rent to pay. In truth, I welcomed not having to prepare for concerts or auditions like an athlete constantly in training.

When practicing for an orchestral flute audition for one of the major symphony orchestras in the U.S that required I learn a difficult Shostakovich Symphony flute part, I started feeling a sense of deep emotional fatigue. All symphony auditions required *note perfection*. You could practice these difficult parts for months, but if one note dropped that day for the judges, you would be quickly eliminated. That just seemed really unfair to me. Although I was in truth very reliable as a performer, these orchestral auditions were simply too geared towards "note perfection" often disqualifying truly fine musicians.

Over a period of eight years, I learned the majority of the orchestral flute repertoire. Throughout my teenage years, I studied with the late, great Harold Bennett (former first flutist of the Metropolitan Opera Orchestra and numerous others.) Even as an older man he could produce a sound on the flute that was as smooth as silk. In lessons he remained in top shape, playing excerpts from Ravel's "Daphnis and Chloe" to Beethoven's "Leonore Overture No. 3" still with a complete command of the instrument. We both played in the style of the French School. In flute terms this meant with a voluptuous vibrato, and more of an effusive, warm and expressive sound.

At the end of high school I auditioned for music colleges with top flute professors around the country. When deciding to study at Oberlin Conservatory of Music (a decision half made by my father who was eager to see me get a "broader liberal arts education" as well as "a true college campus experience") I didn't know that the four years of flute study ahead would be with a teacher from the German School. Mr. Bennett, upon hearing I had decided to study with Mr. Willoughby at Oberlin expressed deep concern over this choice, urging me to rethink my decision. He strongly felt that their teaching styles were quite different.

Robert Willoughby, my teacher at Oberlin Conservatory of Music, was also well known and highly revered in the flute world. I was one of three students in the country selected to study with him that year. Ultimately, Mr. Bennett turned out to be right about their different teaching approaches. Mr. Willoughby taught with a more conservative, emotionally restrained method. His playing did not inspire me, and his tone was not pleasant to listen to.

My desire to play was falling away without my realizing. Spare hours in college were often spent tucked away painting in my dorm room or writing in my journal. I was not like my fellow flute colleagues who were devoting hours in the practice rooms of the conservatory each day. I prepared for my lessons, but cannot recall feeling inspired by them.

Mr. Willoughby was excellent at preparing his students to become orchestral players. Many of the top principal flutists in symphony orchestras throughout the US were his students. And although I learned the majority of orchestral excerpts after four years of study, I believe now, that perhaps I was better suited to becoming a soloist.

Selected as one of three flutists in my senior year at Oberlin, to play in a masterclass for Juilliard professor, Carol Wincenc, I chose the Poulenc Flute Sonata, a piece I had always loved performing. Carol too had studied with both Mr. Bennett and Mr. Willoughby. I adored her recording of the Enesco "Cantabile and Presto," released soon after winning the very prestigious Walter Naumburg Competition. I absolutely loved her playing. Her sound was dark, warm and expressive. I remember attending her NY debut performance at Lincoln Center in my teens, a concert that inspired me deeply. After playing for her, in the greenroom, she asked:

"Where will you be going to grad school?" Taking a deep breath, knowing that I had no plans whatsoever to continue my musical education after college, I replied:

"I just got married to a foreigner from Brazil. My husband and I will be living in New York City right after school."

In a kind manner, she said, "I would like you to study with me. I will teach you privately in my New York apartment."

As it turned out, for a short period of time, once settled into my domestic life in Queens and commuting routine, I took a few flute lessons with Carol in her Upper West Side apartment. It was a great privilege to study with her. After just two lessons she said while on my way out the door:

"You have what it takes, Kim." Words I had not heard for four years at Oberlin Conservatory of Music.

But those endless days behind reception desks in midtown Manhattan in the corporate world, and on subway trains to and from my apartment in Queens left little energy or desire to prepare for lessons. In retrospect, after four uninspired years working with Mr. Willoughby, I was tired.

At the end of every Manhattan workday, I sat quietly for hours at my kitchen table immersed in painting floral textile designs, while my husband Marcelo, studied his astrology peacefully beside me. I somehow found the energy for that.

An Insurance Company

My very first job in New York City was at 18 East 48th Street on the 18th floor at an insurance company, a small office employing eleven people. I was hired to sit behind a small desk, politely answering the phone and typing the occasional business letter.

My desk faced an empty wall just a few feet away. I really had no secretarial skills. I had never even used an electric IBM typewriter before. Every day, the hours passed slowly as if in retrograde motion. Lunchtime with my Brazilian husband became the best part of the day, as it was a chance to get outside and breathe. I felt alive in the city streets. Kathy, my blonde, Catholic schooled boss, a nice woman who took her position very seriously, hoped that I would do the same. She believed in me and had higher expectations than I was ultimately able to deliver. What looked like a simple receptionist job to her was actually intimidating to me. When asked to pull insurance file folders quickly from a room filled with metal cabinets, I felt panicked and overwhelmed. Thank goodness for Greg, the hired computer geek who helped me quickly to locate all of her requests. Kathy always seemed to think it would be helpful for me to actually read through the content of these insurance files, to get better acquainted with their company policies. Nothing seemed duller than that to me.

I only lasted four months in that first job. I remember Mr. David, the company CEO whose cigar hung from his lips, circling the office floor while puffing away. On occasion he extended himself in a friendly manner when passing my desk, but I do recall him watching me type on the IBM with two fingers and asking Kathy, "Couldn't we do any better than this?" My ears went back like a scolded dog. Four months later I was fired. I cried when I got to street level that day where Marcelo was lovingly waiting for me. "I'm a failure. I couldn't keep my first job. Now how will we pay our rent?" I said with tears falling. "You are not a failure, honey," he said. "You are a musician. Musicians do not belong in insurance companies."

High Fidelity

With a degree in Flute Performance on my resume, I decided to try and find work going forward in a music-related environment. My next job was at High Fidelity Magazine / Musical America, as an "Assistant Editor" in the classical music LP- reviewing department.

Amazed that out of one hundred resumes that my father and I had sent out together to various music companies in Manhattan, one job opportunity surfaced. I was eager to work in an office that utilized my knowledge of classical music.

This position presented me with an introduction to a number of skills again unfamiliar to me. I learned how to use a Xerox machine. I filed literally hundreds of dusty archival black and white photos of great musicians such as: Arturo Toscanini, Jascha Heifetz, Maria Callas, and Enrico Caruso and countless others dating back to the turn of the 20th century; copy-editing and spell checking classical LPs, tapes and eventually CDs that had come into the office for review.

Tom was the Senior Editor of the magazine. He was a tall, thin, hard-working employee, always intently reading something behind his typewriter. However, Tom was not my boss. My boss was Roxanne, Tom's secretary. Every morning Roxanne would leave a pile of mail on my desk to open and distribute with a look in her eye that clearly indicated I stay put at my desk.

The joy of each morning however came from Mr. Singh, an eighty-five year old Indian mailman who rolled a grocery cart around the office floor delivering the morning mail to each station. Every day he would greet me warmly, smiling and looking kindly into my eyes. A Buddhist, he introduced me to the idea of past lives and told me:

"My dear, you are a very old soul."

He held and read my palm telling me I would have "many small ailments throughout my life but nothing really insurmountable."

He put cold water gently upon my eyelids one morning to help ease a headache that I had, and gave me licorice seeds to hold between my teeth to cure an upset stomach. These sweet morning exchanges were always the perfect start to a day, until Roxanne arrived.

After a few months of employment, Tom, the Sr. Editor, formally introduced himself and opened conversation. When he discovered that I had graduated with a degree in Flute Performance from Oberlin Conservatory of Music, we shared in –depth conversations about various classical musicians, new recordings he had received for review. This was when the job started to get interesting.

One afternoon Tom approached me with a stack of records in hand.

"Take these home and when you have a chance Kim, give them a listen and tell me your thoughts. I'd like to know what you think of them," he said.

I was quite pleased that my classical music knowledge might now be put to some good use. I carried the pile of CDs and tapes home happily, anxious to return with my critique of them. This led to further dialogue between us. But soon after, I was banished to the back stock room where Roxanne asked that I organize and alphabetize literally thousands of dirty and dusty vintage photos from the Musical America archive. Unable to speak with Tom, and sent to a windowless, dark room of photo files for literally weeks, my lungs filled with archival dust and hands with paper cuts on them, this Editorial Assistant's job went from promising to punishing.

A few months later, while walking down Seventh Avenue on my lunch hour, I came across a sign that read: "National Flute Convention held today at the Sheraton Hotel." My heart started to beat fast. Just as I had finished reading the sign, internationally acclaimed flutist Jean Pierre Rampal whisked by me. A few moments later, Carol Wincenc arrived too. We greeted one another briefly at the entrance. Familiar flute colleagues were swiftly entering the Sheraton Hotel to attend this Flute event. I stood outside wondering whether I should go in too as I only had an hour for lunch.

Soon I was in the lobby. All kinds of flute-related announcements were posted such as: flute lectures, flute concerts, and mock flute orchestral auditions. With just thirty minutes left on my lunch hour, I entered a large room where I sat in the back row watching two of my former flute colleagues from college in a stiff competition. They were both my age. I had performed for years beside them in orchestras and in summer residence at Tanglewood. They were competing in the final round of a mock- orchestral audition before the former first flutist of the New York Philharmonic, Julius Baker.

Sitting nervously for them both while they were each asked to play the most difficult and well known orchestral flute parts in the repertoire before hundreds of fellow flutists, I was glad not to be in their shoes. I could finger these familiar flute parts as they played. I wondered which one of them would drop a note first while displaying a brilliant command of the instrument. Both were equally fine musicians. Both in my opinion deserved to sit Principal Flute in any major orchestra.

When the winner was announced, I was not surprised. Lance and I had been flute colleagues for four years at Oberlin Conservatory of Music. He was a polished musician, always technically on top of his game, precise, and extremely focused. He had poise, grace and admirable confidence, playing with an absolute command of the instrument that almost seemed super human to me. The runner up was a flutist I had spent summers with at Tanglewood and competed with in numerous New York competitions all throughout my youth. Both were worthy of any prize, but I knew that one of them would ultimately be eliminated.

When the mock audition ended, I dashed out the back of the room like Cinderella onto Seventh Avenue. I had literally only five minutes left on my watch to get back to my office desk. It was an unusual lunch break in the midst of a typical work weekday. I knew for sure that I was not envious of the pressures that these fellow flute colleagues were under when competing, but returning to a desk piled high with papers to file, also didn't feel good. All I could think about was The Sheraton Hotel full of familiar flute colleagues right down the block who like a herd of elephants were all moving on without me.

The only one in that office who had any idea of my musical background was Tom. However sadly, Tom's enthusiasm towards me ultimately became the nail in my coffin.

After a year in that job on 7th Avenue and 53rd St. I was fired. I remember clearly that morning how Roxanne came to my desk smiling and said:

"You have an hour to say goodbye and pack up your things." I was completely blind-sided. It had come as a total shock to me that morning.

Tom whisked past my desk with his head down headed towards his office as if he wanted no part of it. I went to visit the magazine's jazz editor, Nancy, who had become a friend. She hugged me goodbye and wished me well. I visited Mr. Singh in the mailroom on my way out, who told me:

"I know what happened my dear. Roxanne tried to get me fired too for talking with too many people in the office and had my route changed. Here is my home phone number. I'd like you and your husband to come have dinner in Queens with my family. We will make you a delicious Indian feast."

Musical Indignities

My next job was at a small but significant Music Management company around the corner from Carnegie Hall. It was right down the block from the venerable Patelson Music House that sadly no longer exists. I remember browsing those old wooden shelves one afternoon looking for a flute part and standing right beside Rudolph Nureyev. He was clad in everything you would wish to have seen this Russian Adonis ballet dancer cloaked in. He wore a billowing peasant blouse with plum velvet vest and Romeo-like vintage coat. On his head, a turban wrapped like a sultan against his sculpted features. Just a few inches away, he looked more handsome than ever.

My next job in Manhattan was at a Music Management on West 54th Street - an old-world company representing many of the now deceased musical legends such as: Victor Borge, Eartha Kitt, Cab Calloway, Doriot Anthony Dwyer, and Abbey Simon. I got this job because my mother, a fine pianist, who had interviewed Victor Borge in his Connecticut home, had connections to his management company. The office to my memory had little daylight. It was furnished with old, shabby pieces of furniture, and a back room graveyard heaped with antiquated typewriters and early computers that today might be considered serious collector's items.

My job there was to occasionally type Press Releases for the upcoming performances and do general, light secretarial work that barely utilized my knowledge of classical music. My boss had a very thick LI accent and horrendous pronunciation of classical composers. "Can you get me the CHICK-OWSKI (Tchaikovsky) tape off the shelf?" he would loudly ask. He and I were face to face all day long, my desk flush up against his. I didn't have an ounce of privacy. My typewriter was such a relic that it had no erase key. I had to use small waxy pieces of paper to erase my frequent typos. My hands were usually covered in typewriter ink.

I dreaded coming to work each morning. I watched my boss feet away, sloppily eating his bagel, simultaneously speaking to me about what he wanted me to do that morning, while chunks of doughy "shrapnel" were flying out.

Many of the artists would come to the office to discuss their upcoming appearances and promotion. One incident really didn't sit well with me when renowned concert pianist Abbey Simon entered the office infuriated. Apparently the program our office had submitted to The New York Times had been incorrect. He was to play at Damrosch Park outside of Lincoln Center. The only other secretary in the office (who was not a musician) had incorrectly typed and submitted Mr. Simon's program. I had never been given any such programs to type. But on that day while walking through the main sitting room where Mr. Simon was angrily giving my boss a piece of his mind, I was suddenly the Fall Guy. In front of this famous concert pianist, I was blamed for something I had not done.

One afternoon, an old violinist friend and colleague with whom I had spent two summers at Tanglewood, entered the office seeking potential management. Joel and I had played together in the orchestra at Tanglewood under the baton of Leonard Bernstein. He was a talented violinist. We had been good friends during those beautiful summers.

"What the hell are YOU doing HERE?" Joel asked in astonishment when seeing me seated behind the old typewriter.

With head down, I replied, "I have no idea, Joel." It was that day that I felt that I couldn't stand being there much longer. I felt uncomfortable seeing my music colleague Joel again. He was a reminder of my rich, musical past and happiest summers of my life.

To make matters worse perhaps, the former first flutist of the Boston Symphony Orchestra, came one afternoon to the office with her flute to "warm up." She was scheduled to play a concert at Lincoln Center. Only four years prior, I had been a Sr. in high school, traveling around the country taking flute auditions at top music schools such as The Curtis Institute of Music, Boston University, Oberlin Conservatory of Music and New England Conservatory, auditioning for colleges with the top flute teachers in United States. She was considered one of the best flute teachers in the world, only accepting three new flute students out of hundreds in her studio, who had auditioned to study with her.

I remember the audition with her very well. I had played the Francis Poulenc Sonata and Bach E Minor Flute Sonata accompanied by my mother at the piano. Atypically, she took me aside after the audition and said sternly:

"You will be one of my three flute students, but you must accept my offer to teach you right *now*." I couldn't do that as I had three more college auditions ahead of me at other top music schools and was not yet decided.

I ultimately wound up studying with Robert Willoughby at Oberlin. But that day behind my typewriter, years later at the music management, while listening to her playing Debussy's "Syrinx"- a piece I had played all my life from memory, a soliloquy based upon the story of Pan, I felt my heart sinking to my feet while tears filled my eyes. When I went into the back room to greet her and remind her of my audition four years prior, she did not remember it.

That job in truth, came with very few musical perks. However, another memorable encounter was when my boss asked me to host an important jazz event at the Parker Meridian Hotel's Penthouse one evening. Many of the greatest jazz musicians were going to attend that night. I personally knew nothing about jazz. I only knew of Winton Marsalis who played on the Tonight Show with Johnny Carson. Asked to dress nicely and be at the hotel at 7:00pm to greet and keep a list of the attendees, I stood behind a wooden lectern with pen and pad writing the names of the jazz musicians who came through the door. It was when one man stepped up that things got a little uncomfortable. When asking for his name, he shouted angrily:

"You don't know who I am???"

I was soon told that I had just pissed off the great Miles Davis. So after just a few months, on a hot summer's day when I would have preferred to be roaming the New York City streets freely, I was again fired. I am not surprised that arriving at the office that particular morning in blue jeans, t-shirt and sandals, (not my usual required formal secretarial attire) must have inspired it.

I'm sorry Mr. Netanyahu

Finding a job in Manhattan was never too difficult for me; somehow even with secretarial skills that were far from stellar. The truth is, over time, my two little fingers learned to type rather fast. I could knock out cleanly executed letters and my confidence improved where administrative work was concerned.

My next post was at a stock brokerage on the East Side of town on 3rd Avenue and 53rd Street, a position completely unrelated to music. That actually refreshed and pleased me. The new job would not be a constant reminder of a musical career I had parted ways with. I was now plain and simply, a receptionist for a fancy stock brokerage, sitting at a posh antique mahogany desk with leather top. To my left was a wall-sized gorgeous Renaissance floral oil painting that looked as if plucked straight out of the Metropolitan Museum of Art. This magnificent floral work of art had my attention every morning. The corporate world was colorless, so I welcomed its presence and decorative beauty. It was lit perfectly and the colors sparkled like jewels.

I accepted the job after one interview, knowing full well that answering a telephone all day in a large open, brightly lit space, would be a welcome change from sitting in a dingy and dark office under my old boss's nose.

What I didn't know when accepting the job was that the company president was a well-known Jewish philanthropist. He was eighty-nine or so at the time, always hunched over with black coat and Magritte-like hat and cane. Each morning I assisted him in removing his heavy coat and hanging it in the front closet. When he discovered I was Jewish, he greeted me with greater warmth.

But one day he took me aside, producing an expensive Gucci white pocket book studded in pearls. "This is for you," he said crouched over and smiling. I wasn't sure what to make of this gesture. When I opened the Gucci purse I was shocked to find it had been stuffed with money. "Vould you like to come to my apartment and see my Degas painting?" he asked. I took a breath, smiling politely, hardly knowing what I was going to say next. "I really appreciate your gift, but I cannot accept it. I also cannot visit your Degas painting even though I love Degas," I admitted. "Yes, of course you can come and see my Degas," he insisted. "Please accept my gift, it's for the holidays," he said warmly pushing the Gucci bag into my hands as if it was a done deal.

Later on in the day when he was leaving the office and I was putting his heavy coat back on, I gently handed the Gucci pearl studded bag back to him, thanking him again, and telling him as firmly as I could, that as much as I very much appreciated his generosity, I could not accept it.

Another morning one of his closest friends, then Israeli Diplomat, Benjamin Netanyahu, walked through the glass front door. He arrived with two security guards on each side. He was not yet the Prime Minister of Israel. He was quite a handsome man. However, my complete lack of political knowledge in my early twenties, led to a slightly embarrassing encounter. Mr. Netanyahu stepped forward. "Kindly announce that Mr. Netanyahu is here." I had never heard the name "Netanyahu" before. Not only had it been spoken quickly, but I also could not make the name out clearly. "Could you please kindly repeat your name, sir?" I asked politely. "Mr. Netanyahu," he said, even more impatiently. Unfortunately, not even with a highly attuned musical ear, was I able at that moment to grasp his name clearly and announce his arrival. Taking a deep breath, I said softly, "I apologize sir, but I wasn't able to make out your name clearly." He then shouted, "Just say that BEN is here!"

This job lasted one year, surprisingly. The pay was steady and the only thing I truly liked about it was the magnificent floral painting beside my desk. I was simply grateful for *any* connection to beauty and art in the cold, corporate world during those years. Everything else seemed cold and lifeless to me. And although everyone at the stock brokerage treated me kindly, I started to feel something changing inside me and I left that job.

Turning Point

The summer after leaving the stock brokerage job was truly a turning point for me. I spent the next six weeks enrolled at Queens College in my very first oil painting class and a Color Theory course. I had not officially graduated from Oberlin College Conservatory of Music by the end of my fourth year. I had made a promise to my father (who had generously paid for my college education) that I would soon after graduation, earn the remaining credits needed to complete my college degree.

I fell in love with oil painting. No class I had ever taken at Oberlin College over the course of four years while earning my degree in music felt as joyful as these two art courses did. I sat in the summer grass on campus with brushes and palette sensuously moving pigment under a sunny sky.

I had actually never taken a single art class in my life. My oil painting teacher, Antonio, a dark and handsome, Italian painter who resembled a young Amadeo Modigliani, and whose own work looked to my eyes a lot like the work of Roualt, headed a class of about twenty students. Each of us had an easel and left to our own devices for three hours, were to paint the still life he had thoughtfully created in the center of the room. I knew my paintings looked very different from everyone else's work once finished. Because I had no formal art education, I didn't know how to paint objects in perspective. I painted these still lives to the best of my ability. Antonio's silence after looking over my work each week often left me feeling uneasy about what I had produced. He would only sometimes gently suggest bringing more light into a painting here or there, but for the most part, he remained silent while watching me paint.

Our final exam at the end of the six-week class was to paint three different canvases: a still life, a room interior, and an outdoor scene. I was eager to paint them all. As a child, looking at art books with my mother of Vuillard, Bonnard and Matisse, whose interiors were layered with rich patterns in sumptuous hues, I felt most inspired to tackle the room interior assignment first; layered with patterns on Oriental rugs, pillows and wallpaper, grand piano, and some French doors overlooking greenery. It was my personal homage to one of my favorite French painters of interiors, Edouard Vuillard. Feeling excited with the end result, I literally jumped in my old Buick and drove the painting out to Long Island (still wet) in the backseat to show to my mother who also loved the work of Vuillard.

When I arrived, I took the canvas out of the backseat carefully. My mother looked closely at it for a few minutes.

"Kim," she said, "I am sorry you drove all the way out here to show me your new painting. I know you were excited to share it with me, but, the room interior is not painted in proper perspective."

She went on to point out what was incorrect about it: my coffee table and grand piano were too small, explaining that only the great painters of the world, who had learned to first paint in proper perspective, then, had the "liberty" to distort it.

I remember how unhappy I had felt hearing her say this. In my own defense I replied:

"Does everything have to be in perfect perspective to be a successful work of art?" Admittedly, that day, I drove back to Queens deeply disappointed.

I loved my Color Theory class at Queens College. The professor was a former student of renowned artist and color theorist, Josef Albers who had designed this course. She told me:

"I want to keep all of your assignments for future classes, Kim. Albers would have loved your work."

These color assignments using paint and Color Aid paper to illustrate the various influences colors had upon one another came as naturally to me as breathing. By the end of the six weeks at Queens College I received my grades for the two painting courses I had taken. I was totally surprised when receiving an A+ from both my oil painting, and Color Theory teachers.

After spending a summer painting, I soon realized there was no going back to the gray, colorless corporate world. I held a few more temp jobs here and there. But it was in a building on Lexington Avenue and 53rd Street, on my way to another grey insurance company where I found myself more clearly at an emotional precipice.

In the lobby of a newly constructed modern building a large art installation by Frank Stella stood directly over the elevators at ground level. You couldn't miss it. Each morning before going to my temp job, I would spend just a few minutes in the lobby gazing up quietly at this large, colorful work before stepping foot in the elevator. It was full of exuberant color and its wonderful energy lifted my wilting spirit. I wondered what it would feel like to make a living in New York doing what I loved most, painting.

The Children's Museum

The very last secretarial job that I held at that time was on West 54th Street off of 8th Avenue working for the first Children's Museum of Manhattan. The space was a creative haven for kids, an odd sort of place where children interacted with iguanas, guinea pigs and hands-on art projects and small interactive exhibits. The space was surprisingly darkly lit, not full of light the way one would hope a children's environment would be.

One of the Museum Directors, a millionaire socialite in New York City, asked me whether I'd like instead to work for her in her duplex apartment on Central Park West rather than at the museum. Her very young daughters had taken a liking to me when visiting the museum. I found the offer appealing and accepted. I figured anything but sitting all day at a desk in a darkly lit place would be preferable. I remember that initial moment of awe when entering her duplex apartment overlooking Central Park. She owned a number of beautiful original Milton Avery paintings that were hanging in her living room. This kind of wealth in New York was new to me at twenty -six. The apartment was bigger than the Colonial house I had grown up in on Long Island. I was mostly required to babysit her young daughters, run an errand to get groceries, and occasionally log information into her office computer there. That didn't seem too bad. The time went by easily, and I was glad not being tied to a desk all day.

It was during that time that the sudden death of my high school boyfriend threw me emotionally off balance, and ultimately, into the arms of a co-worker at the museum. His death had a devastating emotional impact upon me, and a co-worker at the museum lent me his ear and support. In truth, my husband of five years and I had lived a pretty peaceful and loving existence in Queens, with little strife. But restless and disenchanted with my very mundane, predictable existence in Queens; with hours spent commuting by subway every day to jobs that offered no way out from under corporate lights, and perhaps the need to grieve the loss of the death of my high school boyfriend with someone who would listen, I soon found myself ending that first marriage, leaving for Europe with this co-worker, and saying goodbye to my Manhattan years of unfulfilling corporate life.

A New Life in Belgium

I arrived with my suitcases in Belgium in late August. Mitch was already there waiting. I had no idea how I might earn a living in a new country. I felt like a young girl in a Henry James novel. Everything excited me visually. Mitch taught art to children at the International School of Brussels.
We had shared a beautiful Belgian brownstone apartment overlooking a lushly- wooded park and schoolyard. The little town we lived in was called Bois Fort, just a twenty-minute tram ride to the center of Brussels from our front door. I was totally enchanted by everything around me. I was living a dream.

Everywhere I turned there was beauty. Our little town was full of cobblestone streets lined with typically charming Belgian houses and brownstones. I adored seeing the school children in their blue and white uniforms each morning out my kitchen window, walking in single file like Madeleine, down our intimate block. The church bells rang a few times daily out my arched living room windows sending resonant waves of joy through my heart each and every time they chimed.

Our lives together in Belgium were full of adventure, spontaneity and freedom. Every week we were hopping trams and boarding trains to new neighboring towns and countries. We ventured like new lovers, spending every dime we had in our pockets until they were empty. My ears were filled with the lyricism of French, a language I had studied in school for ten years, that I was pleased to be able to put into practice. Initially, I felt nervous going alone to the local grocery store where no one spoke any English; quickly learning new words like "*trenche*" when asking to please cut a chunk of cheese into "slices." These were basic words I had never been taught in school. Every day I forged sweet connections with the local Belgian shopkeepers and found my way around by tram to get to the center of Brussels. I was invited one afternoon to have a friendly glass of "*Maison*" with a handsome restaurateur named Henri. Our light-hearted conversations in my small town helped improve my confidence in French.

I soon got offered a part time job teaching the flute at the International School of Brussels. My flute -teaching schedule was light and sporadic, not demanding, When not at the school, I was home painting textile designs on silk, or exploring the winding cobblestone streets of my charming zip code.

I was happiest spending time in Paris and in Holland; driving aimlessly through the French countryside with Mitch. Trips to chateaus and little cathedral towns every other weekend, past fields of brilliant red poppies, spoke deeply to my painter's heart. On one occasion, at my spontaneous request, we pulled the rental car over to the side of the country road so that I could run wild in a field of poppies.

I also loved Holland with its charming canals and flatlands, fields of brightly colored tulips. We explored The Hague, Amsterdam, Rotterdam, and Delft, marveling at the delicate lace curtains in all of the windows along the canals while happily indulging in the multi-cultural cuisine offered at intimate cafes.

The first official adventure we took together was to Bruges, the city known as "The Venice of the North." It was one of the most beautiful cities I had ever been to in my life. We felt as if in a fairytale, crossing romantic footbridges over shimmering canals framed by brick-colored huddled rows of medieval architecture. It was there that Mitch bought me an old, vintage turquoise ring at an outdoor flea market and spontaneously on one knee, got down and proposed to me alongside a canal. People watched him and a few applauded.

Back in our little hometown of Bois Fort, we took long Sunday walks into the woods surrounding our brownstone apartment where the tall, thin anatomies of trees reminded me of Elliot Porter's photographs of illuminated forests. We would walk through the deep woods for hours, often getting lost while following a single footpath that would eventually lead us to some small, unfamiliar cathedral town. We rested on the front steps of a church, typically eating fresh Brie on baguettes with a hot cup of coffee not knowing where we were, and being totally OK with that.

The Grande Place, at the heart of Brussels, framed by elegant architecture with cafes serving waffles and *moules* (mussels) we explored frequently. We combed flea markets in different cities from Gent to Antwerp, Paris to Amsterdam, carting small, vintage, European treasures with which to brighten our lovely Belgian home. Sporting a new pair of shiny black leather shoes in Paris, he had bought for me, with Pilgrim –like buckles on top, we walked through Place Des Voges and over the Pont Neuf as if walking on air. I couldn't believe this was my new life- so full of beauty, love and adventure.

Renting cars almost every weekend to new undiscovered places, and renewing our visas by driving over the border in to Germany, I remember instantly feeling much less moved by the colder facades of the German architecture. We visited Beethoven's birthplace in Bonn, a stunning experience, incredulously gazing at the keys of his clavier. It was easy for me to imagine how life had been during Mozart and Beethoven's times as we walked through a square that seemed as if it had not really changed much over the centuries. However, in truth, I missed Belgium's heavier, rustic peasant- type of architecture. Whether by tram, car or train to neighboring countries, our wanderlust was insatiable.

In between these weekend excursions, while Mitch was at work, I spent countless hours alone at my dining room table, painting hundreds of silk textile designs. Before leaving New York, I had taken a quick silk painting course at the Fashion Institute of Technology. And although just a brief introduction to the medium, I fell in love with its vibrant color saturation and smooth and sensual surface quality.

During the day, I quietly painted silk floral designs that Dani, a professional seamstress whose business was run from her basement, turned into pillow covers and scarves. We smoked freshly rolled cigarettes and in French shared a mutual love for astrology. She gave me the name of her astrologer who days later read my natal astrological chart. In a very thick French accent the astrologer said:

"You love to *heave*." "Heave?" I asked incredulously.

"Yes, *heave, heave*." she said again. I asked her to spell the word on a small piece of paper. She spelled the word "*give*."

I explained to her the difference in English between "heave" and "give" and we both laughed.

"You have a Grand Trine in Water between the signs of Pisces, Cancer and Scorpio," she said. "This means you are a creative genius. Don't have children. You were meant to give the world your creativity. With this Grand Trine, you must focus on creating beauty for the world," she said.

During that time I formed a musical trio of flute, violin and piano with musicians from the International School of Brussels. We gave concerts in chateaus and at the school. Although I was happy to still be playing my flute now and then, I felt myself emotionally drifting away from the instrument and desire to perform. Unwilling to practice long hours during my spare time, and distracted by my thirst for travel and painting, concertizing felt like a chore. I had grown comfortable with my creative freedom and no-demands European existence. Mitch was a wonderful travel companion, always full of good humor, adventure and laughter coming up with colorful excursions to surrounding countries that I eagerly went along with.

And after a year in an enchanted European chapter of my life, so full of creative freedom and beauty, adventure and musical opportunities, engaged to Mitch (whom I ultimately wound up parting ways with), I returned to New York City, about to enter one of the darkest chapters of my life.

Coming Home

Mitch and I traveled back to New York for a few weeks to reconnect with family. He had a short freelance job awaiting him. I was not sure what I would be doing while he was employed. It didn't take much time however for me to fall right back into my city stride. I missed certain cultural things about my American life. Long summer walks along Broadway on the Upper West Side with my best girlfriend Sharon, rekindled my love of New York.

Europe had all the beauty in the world to offer but Manhattan spoke to my all-too American need for instant gratification. I could let me hair down in the New York City streets. Just the simple desire for a greasy hamburger in the middle of the day at Big Nick's along Broadway (which is sadly no longer there) excited me. In my small Belgian village restaurants always seemed to be closed when my hunger pangs kicked in. Most of them only opened for dinner at 7:00pm.

In denim, t-shirt and sandals the American girl was now home again in her beloved city; feeling fancy-free. The beauty of Europe was of course, unparalleled. I was no longer hearing church bells out my windows, but New York offered energy, diversity and color in a way that I had to admit I had missed.

I didn't want to return to Belgium. I had no idea how I would earn money in New York City, or how I would support myself, but the city was calling me back home to stay.

A Kite Without A String

Single and unemployed in Manhattan, with no job prospects on my horizon whatsoever, I realized the choice I had just made to return would come with some all-too familiar financial and emotional challenges. I knew for sure that I didn't want to work again in the corporate world. Now occupying a small studio apartment on East 81st Street meant paying rent again. The following months were a strand of temping jobs, positions held in various companies like HBO, the UN translating French documents, and working at a t-shirt company across from Radio City Music Hall.

Briefly dating a handsome actor of Irish and Italian decent who was a bartender by night, I soon found myself in another romantic relationship. James was charming, witty and spontaneous. We shared a similar sense of humor. I could tell that despite our magnetic chemistry and gift for gab, he had to cut ties, surrendering to his family's very strict religious views. The relationship ended three months later when he told me:

"I could never marry you because you're not Catholic. I couldn't even introduce you to my parents." Well that ended that.

While looking for work, I decided to interview at another employment agency in New York City expressing interest in finding a "textile position." I thought this might lead me in the direction of a more creative and artistic job, but instead, I was sent on an interview at a t-shirt-manufacturing company for another administrative secretarial job.

The interview process seemed to go on forever. I must have been called back five times for a corporate job I knew in my gut I would ultimately wind up leaving for the same reasons I never lasted at any of the others. Every young woman seated in the waiting room had a shiny, black briefcase and matching black heels. All looked like they had a much better chance at getting that secretarial position than I did. Once again unfortunately, I won the audition.

I'd been interviewed by Robert, a freshly divorced, forty-something balding man who angrily punched his fist against the surface of his desk when speaking to me about his ex-wife behind his closed office door. I listened politely. I disliked his aggressive behavior and knew that going forward any work done with him would probably not result well.

Dressed up in heels and corporate attire, I was yet again at another desk in a small office, in a room with no windows and dark wooden paneling. Months of paperwork had now amassed upon an ugly Formica desktop awaiting my arrival. I was supposed to sort through and organize all of the papers before the company President returned.

One of my biggest problems on any job I had ever held was that I did everything too fast. No one seemed to appreciate my ability to complete work in a timely manner. What looked like a week's worth of paperwork for most people, I guess, was usually a day's work for me. One afternoon, Robert found me sitting idly at my desk. With an angry voice he asked:

"So should I assume that you have nothing to do?"

The President arrived a week later. He was a heavyset Orson Wells look-alike, a friendly man. He was the typical 1950s type boss looking subordinately upon all women as secretaries. He called me into his office.

"I need you to take a letter in short hand," he said.

I guess he thought this was a secretarial skill I possessed, but I didn't. It was not on my resume. Smiling politely and sitting in a leather armchair directly in front of his desk after work office hours, I took out my yellow pad scribbling faster than a speeding bullet while he dictated what turned out to be a five-page letter. By the end of the second page, my hand was severely cramped and I couldn't move it any further. Although he kept on dictating the letter, not noticing me at all, my pretend-shorthand session had clearly stopped long before. I smiled, appearing to be a perfect secretary while nodding my head throughout the dictation of his letter. When he finally looked up he said:

"I hope you got all of this down. You can read the letter back to me in the morning. You can go home now."

Tomorrow never actually arrived at that office for me. I called the next morning to say that I would no longer be coming in to work. There was simply no way to magically produce a letter he had dictated the night before. It was my perfect escape route and excuse.

And just one week after that ended, I was already working at the Lincoln Center Metropolitan Opera House Gift Shop. For $7 an hour, I found myself recommending classical recordings and selling opera paraphernalia, speaking three languages with foreign music lovers who came through the front doors. I enjoyed sharing my classical music knowledge, but most of the hours were spent on my feet behind the shop's glass display counter. There was no stool to sit on for more than eight hours a day. The low pay was not covering my rent. That job didn't last long either.

ECHO Chamber

Years back, when painting silk scarves, I wondered if I might find some kind of employment in New York City where I could paint or design, even though I had absolutely no training, resume or degree from F.I.T., Parsons School of Design or SVA. I met with an employment agency around the corner from Grand Central Station, and showed a few scarves while being interviewed there. I literally had a case full of them, created over the years. My resume offered no professional design experience, only corporate jobs briefly held. Anyone could see that I never lasted long at any of these companies.

The agent filed my resume away in a drawer with the words, "She paints beautiful silk scarves" written boldly in black ink across the top of it. Years later, another agent pulled it out of the files and called me.

"Do you still paint silk scarves?" she asked.

"Yes, I do," I said.

"If you are interested, I have a job here at a well-known scarf company for an Associate Designer's position. Can you come in today so that we can discuss it?"

I knew of this scarf company. My mother owned many of their silk scarves.

Two years before I received this call, in sub zero winter weather, I waited on a long line outside of the Henri Bendel department store on what was called their "open market day." Hundreds of young, hopeful, nameless designers like myself brought their original fashion creations to show the Henri Bendel buyers in the hope of having them be carried at the famed retailer.

After four long and frigidly cold hours standing in high heels on 5th Avenue, huddled against one my best friends who generously agreed to accompany me that day, I finally made it through the side door. With frozen hands and feet, I could barely open my two cases to display my silk hand painted scarves.

The buyer was a pleasant middle-aged woman who said, "These are beautiful, but are they colorfast?" (This was a term I didn't know until meeting her.) "Colorfast" meant that the colors would not run if wet or washed. Since all of my scarves had been hand painted with liquid dyes, they would unfortunately bleed when wet. In a kind manner she said, "I think you should design silk scarves. Here is the name of a well-known company here in the city that produces them. I should think they would hire you in a heartbeat in their design studio." She then scribbled the name of this well-known scarf company down on a piece of paper with her contact person there.

I followed up immediately and set up an appointment. When I arrived at the scarf company, I was led into a small, brightly lit conference room. Asked to set my work up on a long conference room table, I carefully laid each of my hand painted silk scarves out under florescent lights. The lights brought their colors to vivid life like jewels.

Marta, a small, brown curly-haired, sixty-something, long-time company employee walked into the room. She walked directly over to the table to have a look at them and said rather quickly:

"What do you want *me* to do with *these*?" I was not sure how to respond.

I asked, "What do you mean?"

"What are these supposed to tell me? I would need at least a year to teach you how to design a silk scarf properly. I don't have time for that. You can put them away now. There's no job for you here," she said dismissively.

So a few years later, when the employment agency near Grand Central Station contacted me about an "Associate Designer's" position where Marta worked, I remembered that bitter encounter with her. I wondered whether she was still working there.

Interviewed three times at length by the scarf company president, a strong-willed matriarch who was running a family business, I was offered the Associate Designer's position.

Marta was still there. She had been the studio manager for some time. She occupied a small office inside the studio itself, the only room with a door that could lock with a key. All the artists in the studio secretly referred to her as "the barracuda." Her office had a window overlooking everyone's drafting tables where she could keep a close eye on what they were doing throughout the day. The studio artists referred to her office with the window as "the shark's cage." Her function was to supervise the designer's scarf layouts and specs. She would often storm out of her office angrily, reprimanding talented, sensitive artists who dared to socialize a little bit on the job. Thankfully, my office was in a separate room down the hall.

My new position required that I meet often with fashion clients along Fifth Avenue, such as: Benetton, GAP, Old Navy, Ann Taylor, Federated, etc. and look for the appropriate scarf artwork that would perfectly accessorize and complement their new collections.

Every morning I faxed numerous factories in China, Korea and Japan with a long list of details for scarf development. I was to make sure deadlines were met and items delivered on time, with colors and executions of these prints I had chosen, accurately executed for the customers. The paperwork was an unending Torah scroll. My desk was heaped every single morning with new designs and fresh faxes from overseas factories all waiting for immediate reply. It was boot camp. I was not hired to paint in the studio or to create an original design. This was not a creative type of position as I had hoped. I was a juggler of a million details for many of their fashion clients. Every day I did my best to stay on top of the mountain of work that awaited me. I somehow managed it all, gaining very important industry knowledge and experience.

One day however, one of the largest pieces of original artwork that had been purchased for a fashion company in England (one of their many clients) that I had left lying across my desk only the night before, quite suddenly, disappeared. By the following morning this large, original piece of artwork was nowhere to be found. Frantically looking everywhere in the office for it, asking fellow employees if they had seen it, no one knew where it was.

My boss Susan, with whom I shared a large bright office overlooking Fifth Avenue, was a nice woman and extremely organized and meticulous person. She was always looking over my shoulder, questioning my perhaps more organic, Aquarian, method of all that was before me. I thought I was handling my workload rather well.

"Kim," she said, "misplacing an expensive piece of artwork is just totally unacceptable. This shows you are not organized. I will have to discuss this with the people upstairs."

I knew right away that my job was in jeopardy. I had to agree that misplacing such a huge piece of artwork was of course unacceptable. I couldn't imagine though what had happened to it.

Unable to defend the disappearance of this huge and costly design, I was soon sent after a year of hard work, "upstairs" for my "exit interview." I was given the chance to "present my case" to the VP of Marketing, even though it seemed clear that a final decision had already been made. I would be let go.

Once fired, and several weeks later, a close artist friend in the design studio, secretly called me at home to tell me that the lost design had "miraculously resurfaced." When I asked her where it had been found, she said, "Locked inside Marta's office."

Painting for a Living

One of the very first painting studio jobs I had was at a Canadian fabric, house on East 39th Street in the heart of the fashion industry. There were five artists in this intimate design studio setting, who were all extremely gifted and lovable people. Among them one Canadian woman, a British and an Indonesian man, a young Korean girl, and I was the token American.

Every day we all sat at our drafting tables painting under florescent lights, talking about our lives, our dreams, and openly admiring each other's artistic fortes.

Everyone there had graduated from some art or design school except for me. The job required a good degree of technical work outside my creative comfort zone. I was asked to repaint intricate equestrian prints, and carefully executed geometric patterns in gouache and dyes. Diana was the head of the studio. She was patient and kind while I learned new painting techniques on the job. A small cassette machine kept things lively in the studio playing all kinds of music while we painted. On any given day one of us would be the designated DJ selecting what we would all be listening to while working. On occasion I even brought my beloved, young golden retriever Maggie to work that added warmth to the studio atmosphere.

Duncan was the British artist in the studio whose fine art paintings reminded me of the work of Jean Dubuffet. His paintings were witty and sophisticated. He had a typical British wry sense of humor that made everyone laugh.

Every painter in the room possessed something special artistically. I was always amazed at how Lizzie and Robby could paint a detailed flower or teacup the size of a thimble to perfection. Diana could knock out textile designs of hunting scenes with wild horses and dogs that almost jumped off the page they were so realistic. And me, I was the one with an exuberant color sense, and looser freehanded approach. Diana gave me floral prints and splashier more impressionistic designs to repaint, patterns that could sell on teenager's bathing suits and youthful active wear.

One morning, I was the designated DJ. I stuck a tape of a flute concert I had given during my Oberlin College years on the deck.

"What's this we're listening to?" Duncan asked blithely.

"It's me," I said. "This was a flute concert I gave a few years ago when I was in college."

Duncan put his brushes down, turned his swivel chair towards mine, raised his eyebrows and said:

"Girl, what the hell are you doing here if you can play the flute like *that*?"

I guess for a few moments his question threw me a bit, until I realized that I was just happy enough now being amid these lovely artists and pushing a paintbrush in New York City for a living.

The studio was really a very pleasant place to come to work. There was so much camaraderie. We had a fair amount of creative freedom, and Diana was a very cool boss. I stayed for almost a year there before moving on to my next painting studio position at another fabric convertor a few blocks away along 6th Avenue, a competitor of theirs who offered me a bit more money. I was sorry to leave the comforts and friendships I had forged at that first studio position behind, but was grateful for the confidence and design education it provided.

In my new painting studio job however, the vibe was completely different. Everyone there was in a creative straight jacket. We weren't allowed to talk to one another while we painted. The head of the studio's name was "Joy" and she was anything but that. No one was free to even mix a single color without her approval. Nothing pleased her. It became harder and harder to come in to work and sit and paint all day long under such rigid direction. The hours of the day felt totally endless to me there. Joy went as far as to collect all of our headphones one morning, the only ounce of escapism or pleasure any of us felt. Trips to the bathroom were getting more frequent, the only moments for any of us to gossip or breathe.

After three months on that job I was called into Joy's office. I knew I was going to get the axe and I welcomed it.

"You wanted this to happen, didn't you?" she asked me.

"Yes kind of, I did," I said looking earnestly into her eyes. "There's no creative freedom here. I don't know how you can expect anyone to produce anything inspired or beautiful, given the way you speak to the artists" I told her.

Joy looked stunned by my honesty. In an uncharacteristically friendly manner, she wished me well and we parted ways.

Benjamin Braddock at the Whitney

During those early painting studio years, it was hard to say what actually felt worse – being in a job all day long that offered little creative freedom, or coming home to my second husband, Harry.

Right after living in Belgium and returning to New York City, I was dating a few creative men ranging from soap opera actors to documentary film producers. I wasn't exactly unhappy. I enjoyed my freedom and colorful social life. I didn't feel any rush to get married again. Perhaps in my mother's eyes, my life seemed like it was going nowhere.

One evening she phoned me about a man from my hometown on Long Island whom she felt would "Provide well for me" and "help you to finally settle down." Reluctantly, I took her advice and went out on my first date with Harry, a matrimonial attorney from my hometown. From our very first date, I felt that we were coming from completely different worlds and I should have trusted that. He pulled up outside my small studio apartment building on East 81st Street in his red Alfa Romeo convertible, top down, a car I had never driven in before. Initially, I suppose, there was some kind of comfort in knowing we'd grown up in the same Long Island zip code, but ultimately, we might as well have been from different planets.

After three months of dating and a fast trip to Barbados together (where I threw my neck out and spent the last few days on my back in agony, a sure sign that I must not have been listening to my gut instincts), I convinced myself that perhaps my mother was right, that it was time for me to settle down. My beloved grandfather, Eddie asked me before the ceremony, "Are you sure doll, that you want to marry him?" a question no bride really wants to be asked on her wedding day. My best friend Sharon, who never liked him, whispered in my ear: "There's still time to run for the hills. You don't have to go through with this." I walked down the aisle as if in a trance, wearing my mother's vintage wedding dress that she'd worn when marrying my father (which should have been an obvious bad omen to me), and said my vows on automatic pilot.

Suddenly the scene of Elaine running out of the church on her wedding day screaming, "Benjamin!" (played by Dustin Hoffman from one of my favorite movies "The Graduate") flashed through my mind. I guess I must have held some degree of hope in my head that after Harry and I got married, things could miraculously improve. I would "settle happily" into this new domestic, suburban Long Island life with a man from my hometown, the way my mother had envisioned, but that never happened.

Harry was usually plastered to the television set on most evenings and weekends at home. He was an avid sports fan. He was a lover of the New York Giants, the Yankees and the Knicks. He had absolutely no desire to share art, astrology, music or anything of interest to me, anyway. If I spoke of astrology, he would roll his eyes impatiently, dismissing it as "total garbage." In truth, we couldn't share anything. If I wanted to listen and sing along to Tori Amos in his Alfa Romeo on the way out to Long Island, he would pop the cassette out without hesitation. Everything became cause for argument.

I spent most nights alone, dancing in tights and tank top in our small living room to Madonna's "Erotica." Plans made with my family members often got cancelled at the last moment when some sports event on television was more important to him. On one such planned family luncheon in Central Park I was left carrying a heavy picnic basket, our 86 lb golden retriever Maggie on a leash, while hailing a taxi to East 69th Street where my father was waiting to meet us after having driven all the way in from New Jersey. Upon arrival, my father looked at me and said angrily:

"Where's the idiot?" I had no way to defend Harry's selfish actions.

"Can we just enjoy ourselves without him, Dad?" I asked.

Those three years of marriage felt like an eternity. I went to see the movies Harry liked, the restaurants most often of his choosing, and did everything possible to keep a degree of peace at home. I had no interest in basketball, but I went to numerous Knicks games anyway with him at Madison Square Garden. My real reason for going though was not to see the Knicks. I had hoped to see Benjamin Braddock – the main character in the movie, The Graduate. Benjamin was a big Knicks fan and was often spotted on the big screen at the games.

During the course of those miserable three years of marriage I actually had the gift of meeting Benjamin on the steps of the Whitney Museum, a star whose photo I secretly had carried around in my wallet for many years.

One afternoon I went with a neighbor of mine to see an Edward Hopper exhibition at the Whitney Museum. It was common knowledge in my family that for years I had been infatuated with Benjamin. He was my fantasy man. Ernie, my stepfather had actually interviewed him at a small movie theatre in Northport, Long Island when the film "The Graduate" had just been released. Benjamin was in his twenties at that time and swiftly becoming a major movie star. Ernie, a film enthusiast, attended this screening speaking briefly with him afterward, and then, snapping a black and white photo on the front steps of the little theatre on his old camera. Decades later, as a loving gesture to me, (and half as a joke) Ernie gave me a black and white 8x10 and wallet-sized copy of his photograph of Benjamin for my birthday. I secretly kept the smaller one in my wallet during those truly miserable years of marriage.

When leaving the Hopper exhibit on the front ramp of the Whitney Museum that day, my friend Linda turned to me and said:

"Hey look Kim! There's Benjamin Braddock!"

Incredulously, I turned around, and there he was in the flesh. My heart was beating out of my chest. A bevy of young women were gathered around him asking for his autograph. I wanted no part of that scene. Mustering my gumption however, I quickly looked through my wallet for the photograph Ernie had given to me. I walked over to him, with hand slightly trembling, tapped him gently on his shoulder and said softly as he was turning around, "Hi, Mr. Braddock, I am sorry to bother you. I have something I would like to share with you, if that's ok?"

Benjamin's face lit instantly up with a smile as he turned toward me. I loved his quick ability to jump right in to any colorful human dynamic. Before I knew it we were having a rather light-hearted flirtation. Pulling this small black and white photo out from my wallet, I said: "I'm not sure I should tell you this, but I have carried this photo of you with me for years, and it was taken by my stepfather in Northport, Long Island, when you made an appearance at a small theatre there to promote your new film, "The Graduate."

Benjamin took the black and white photo from my trembling hand and stared closely at his young face in the photo. He turned to his father standing right beside him on the ramp and said twice aloud:

"Dad, would you look at that? Would you look at that!"

Soon he had his arm around me smiling. My heart was racing.

"Do you have a pen?" he asked me.

"No, I don't think so," I replied while swiftly fishing through my bag for one. "Mr. Braddock, I don't need you to sign my photo. It's not necessary," I said.

"What's your name?" he asked smiling.

After telling him my name, he turned to the group of young women still watching all of this on the ramp, and asked if anyone had a pen. One was then quickly produced. On the back of my small black and white photograph he wrote:

"To Kim, FINALLY!! Love, Benjamin," (along with the date and a big heart drawn beside it.) He kissed me on the cheek as he handed it back to me.

"Have you been in the museum and seen the Hopper exhibit already, Kim?" he asked.

"Yes, I have, the exhibit was amazing," I replied.

"Would you like to see it again with me and my father?" I turned to my neighbor Linda, who by this time was very anxious to return home as she was not actually feeling well that day.

"I am sorry," I said with a burning regret in my gut, "I have to leave with my friend here who isn't feeling well. But thank you for this amazing invitation."

After that, we waved goodbye. Benjamin entered the Whitney Museum. In a state of excitement, I ran to a payphone on the corner of Madison Avenue to call Ernie to tell him what had happened.

"Thank you Ernie!! This never would have happened if you hadn't given me that photo!! You're the best stepfather!!" I said breathlessly. Ernie laughed at the other end of the phone in sheer delight.

Thankfully, three months later, a totally miserable three- year marriage to Harry was finally over. When the day arrived that his many boxes were all moved out, I remember well the deep sense of relief I had felt. The agony was over. Lying beside my golden retriever Maggie, with my feet up on the sofa, in a now almost empty apartment, I smoked a cigarette with that same kind of deep satisfaction and feeling of victory that Paul Newman had when he'd won his case in court in the final scene of "The Verdict."

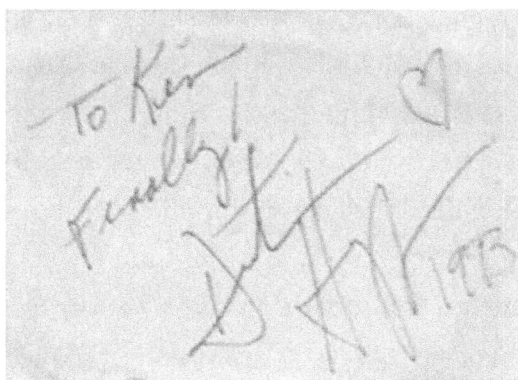

Happy Halloween

During those last few months of my miserable marriage to Harry, something quite miraculous had occurred. A close friend of mine invited me to a Halloween party in the East Village. Weighing a little more than 100 lbs, seriously agoraphobic (due to the anxieties of that abusive relationship) I was not used to going to parties. I had debilitating panic attacks on a daily basis that literally paralyzed me. Some of my friends, who knew me during my carefree European days of adventure, witnessed this dramatic change in me and were incredulous that I was the same person.

One evening while Harry was buried in a New York Giants game with the TV volume up loudly, rejecting the idea to accompany me to a Halloween party, I decided to pull myself together and just go alone. I didn't have a costume. I decided to go to the party dressed in a Jane Austen, 19th century era "Pride and Prejudice" outfit, the only thing I could think of to wear. I had a black velvet French- cuffed dress with white satin collar that I bought when living in Belgium. It had a beautiful vintage quality, and paired with some old lace up leather boots, hair back neatly in a bun, I bravely jumped in a taxicab, heading downtown to this East Village party.

The Halloween party was held at a lovely railroad apartment on East 6th Street between Avenues B& C. It was furnished in tasteful antiques and walls painted with *trompe l'oeils*. Petrified to even speak with any of the guests there due to my anxiety, I gazed across the room at a handsome young man standing in front of an upright piano. Dressed in the absolute male counterpart to my vintage Jane Austen velvet dress, in crisp white shirt and billowing Darcy-like sleeves, I observed him speaking with his guests. He was the host of the party. A few Juilliard musicians were invited to perform. As each guest entered I noticed the refined manner in which he had placed his index finger over his lips, indicating to his guests to enter in quietly while the music was playing. As a classical musician, I was instantly impressed with this sensitive understanding. I was immediately struck by his fine manner that stood in harsh contrast to the person at home with the television up loud watching the Giants.

A bit later I found myself at the stereo while a CD of Brazilian music was playing. That was when he was suddenly right beside me.

"We have not been introduced," he said softly. "My name is Felipe."

We soon discovered that we were both fluent in Portuguese sharing a mutual affection for Brazilian music and connection to the culture. Felipe was half Brazilian.

"Would you like to see my new car?" he asked pleasantly. I accompanied him to the front window of his East Village railroad apartment where he pointed to a second-hand blue VW Rabbit parked below at street level. That second-hand car, (not a red Alfa Romeo), was *my* type of car.

"I love it!" I told him. I explained that I had actually learned how to drive a car in a VW Rabbit while in college and had a special affection for that particular vehicle. And that evening upon arriving home, for the first time in three miserable years, I felt suddenly alive again. I couldn't take my mind off of him.

I took out my journal and started writing about our meeting. I asked the Universe to please help me to find my way out of my bad marriage with

Harry and to please help me meet someone "like Felipe." I knew I could not have him. He was married. But his kindness left a deep impression on me. For a year though, I wrote about him in my journal.

And during the course of that year, Felipe and I ran into each other several times in the streets of New York City. One afternoon while I was returning home from Greenwich Village, avoiding the congestion of the Union Square flower market by walking around its perimeter, there in front of the Barnes and Noble on East 17th Street, I heard a voice calling my name. When I looked over, I saw Felipe smiling.

"I can't believe it, " he said, "I was *just* thinking about you three seconds ago, and now you appeared!"

I was more than delighted to hear him say this. Had the man I had been thinking and writing about secretly in my journal since the day we had met been thinking about me too?

A few weeks later that summer, invited to an outdoor luncheon held in a garden at a Japanese restaurant in the East Village by our same mutual friend, I was offered the only seat left at the far end of the picnic table. "Sit here," Felipe's wife firmly suggested. With no other place for me to sit, I wound up seated right beside him. Every time our legs bumped beneath the table, I felt a surge of electricity coursing through my body.

And one year after my divorce from Harry, the telephone rang.

"Is this Kim?" Felipe asked. "Yes," I replied, "Is this Felipe?" "Yes," he said, "My wife and I have separated. I was just wondering whether I could take you for coffee?"

It was the only night that week that I had actually been home, not out late with friends. Ever since my divorce to Harry I had become much stronger, happier, healthier and more socially active.

"I have to tell you," he said, "I have not stopped thinking about you, Kim, since the day we met at the Halloween party."

We spoke for an hour that night by phone. A few days later he arrived in his blue VW Rabbit with a generous bouquet of yellow roses that he instantly handed to me when I opened his car door.

We lived together for a year, and then we were married. Riding downtown on the New York City subway with little fanfare except for the presence of my closest girlfriend as a witness, in true New York City fashion, we tied the knot. Dressed in the same, elegant, vintage Jane Austen, 19th century novel clothes we'd met in at the Halloween party, we joyfully said our vows in the Municipal Building, with the kind of love in our hearts one hopes to feel on such a day.

The Carriage House Series

When Felipe and I first married, we were living on a shoestring budget in a rent-controlled apartment in Gramercy Park. One morning I was walking past an old carriage house on my street that had always been shut. That morning however, the door was open. A Japanese man greeted me kindly from inside. He was an architect. In the center of the space was a huge drafting table, the type you might only see once in a lifetime. It was the size of a Queen bed in an old wood, museum quality. "Can you use this?" he asked me. I couldn't believe the offer but had to surrender to reality that it wouldn't even fit through the front door of my prewar building, not to mention, my small one bedroom apartment.

"If you see anything in here that you want," he said kindly, "it's yours."

In the corner of the garage, I spotted a thick stack of plain white rice paper as high as my knee. "Are you throwing that paper out?" I asked. "Yes," he said. "Could I possibly have it?" I asked incredulously. "Of course," he said smiling. The paper was thick and heavy. The surface quality was wonderfully rough. There must have been about fifty sheets or more.

This beautiful moment in my life as a painter has never left my memory. I had no easel and no large surface to paint upon other than my living room floor to spread myself over. Like diving into a pool on a hot summer's day,

I took the kind of deep plunge into my paints that was one of the most liberating moments of my artistic life. My unconscious mind and spirit had never been so freely activated. I had the open space upon these pristinely clean white pieces of paper to take chances, to throw myself over their surfaces with the kind of abandon one might imagine flying feels like.

Abstract gardens were coming out of me every day. I cannot remember each one's birth, but I can recall the "feeling" I had when creating this body of work (which I have referred to as "The Carriage House Series.") The gift that had been bestowed upon me that summer's day led to an outpouring of joy that took my work from pure abstraction towards painted gardens -- a clear transition; a bridge I shall never forget crossing.

An Early Exhibit

It was during the first year of our marriage that I started painting larger scaled fine art works on canvas. A former pro, Felipe was teaching tennis at a club in Long Island City. He often hit with many of the top tennis players such as John McEnroe, Virginia Wade, and celebrities such as Liam Neeson and Tom Brokaw.

One afternoon, with a rather substantial body of abstract paintings accumulating in our small, one bedroom apartment, I felt a sudden desire to jump into our Chevy station wagon and drive together to a gallery on Broome Street in Soho. I had recently viewed an amazing black and white Abstract Expressionist exhibit there that haunted me. The works were all visually exciting, reminiscent of Franz Kline's black and white abstract canvases- with energy that literally leaped right off the surface. There was something about that exhibit that inspired me to return to that gallery space a few weeks later with a degree of confidence.

This was a most unusual thing to do in New York City. There were rigid protocols in the gallery world, and most spaces were booked well in advance for shows. Artists with incredibly impressive, long lists of previous gallery exhibitions on their resumes to their credit were usually the ones getting signed on. I had not a single exhibition to show for, and I guess I wasn't afraid of such industry protocols. I just wanted to receive feedback about the work that I was doing, even if it meant a kick in the heart.

We drove to Broome Street in SoHo, in our 88 Chevy wagon with five canvases stacked in the back. I entered the gallery and was soon met by a young blonde assistant named Bradley who greeted me with a smile.

"Can I help you?" he asked cheerfully.

"Yes, maybe," I said. "I saw your last show here with those incredible black and white charcoal works and I was blown away by how beautiful they were. To be honest, I have a car parked outside, full of my own work that I'd love to show the owner of the gallery if that is even possible. I know this isn't the way things are usually done, " I said smiling.

"Did you say you have them in your car?" he asked curiously.

"Yes," I said. "Bring them inside. I'd be happy to take a look." I ran to our old Chevy wagon that was parked right out front. Felipe swiftly carried the heavy stack of five canvases through the gallery door and stood each one up against the clean white wall.

"These are yours?" Bradley asked.

"Yes," I said. "Can you wait here a second? I'd like to grab the gallery owner in the back and show them to him."

A few moments later Keith walked out, a tall, bearded, middle-aged man in flannel shirt and jeans, whose casual, friendly and earthy appearance didn't seem to match my image of the typical New York gallery owner. We greeted one another. He quietly eyed the works that were leaning up against his gallery wall.

"How many of these do you have?" he asked. "I have many," I replied.

Keith walked away and disappeared into the back room and then returned.

"How would you like a show in a month from now? I have an unusual situation. One of my artists got sick and had to cancel her show. There isn't a lot of time, unfortunately. Do you think we could have about twenty-five of your paintings by September? The show would be all yours."

I found myself incredulously committing to a one-woman show in Soho at a gallery on Broome Street. I knew I had enough work already for it. It was a beautiful, deep space, with high ceilings and bright lights that I had imagined (when viewing the black and white show there) could showcase my work beautifully. Cards were soon being printed for the exhibit and mailed shortly after to their clients and friends. The show's opening was under a full moon that late summer's evening. I had never seen my work presented in such a wonderful way, and. I had to walk around the block several times in the course of opening night, just to stay calm.

One morning while the show was still up at the gallery but a week from coming down, Felipe came home from teaching an early tennis lesson.

"How would you like to meet one of the top bestselling criminal mystery writers?" he asked. I honestly didn't know who this writer was at that time. I soon learned she was world famous and her books were in every airport terminal.

"She saw your card announcement taped on my locker at the tennis club. She really liked it a lot," he said. "She would like to come over and see your work when the show comes down. I invited her to come to our apartment next week."

The following week, in our one-bedroom, seven hundred square foot rent controlled Gramercy Park apartment, I somehow managed to open up just enough space in the living room to show her the paintings from the exhibit set against the one white wall we had. She was friendly and open, effusive and generous with her responses to the paintings. Pointing to a few of them she liked, she asked:

"Can you please write me an invoice for these?" With hands shaking and my math skills hitting an all-time low, I could barely add the figures together on paper.

"You'll have to come to my Central Park West apartment and see them hanging," she said while hugging us both affectionately goodbye.

Farewell to 9 to 5

After five years of painting jobs in various fashion studios, I finally managed to earn the kind of creative freedom on the job that I had long hoped to acquire.

Hired as resident "colorist" for a fabric house on 6th Avenue, Lucy, my new Chinese boss, believed in me from the very start. She hired me for my color sense and to design floral patterns that would be converted into yards of fabric. My line was to target a "Junior Market" – a young, teenaged demographic in the fashion industry. These bolts of fabric sold well for the company.

The studio job was strictly 9-5. I sat at a drafting table in a large open room full of painters of all ages doing the same, all of whom were trained in textile design. There were three bosses. One of them, a Zsa Zsa Gabor look-alike with a high bouffant cotton candy blonde hairdo had a bit of an abrupt approach when directing the studio artists. With me however, she was friendly. One afternoon when one of her artists took the day off, during one of her emotional tirades, she handed me a design to repaint in a technique that was clearly out of my technical comfort zone. Lucy, my boss, quickly came to my rescue that morning saying:

"Kim is not a copy machine! She is an artist. Give that technical work to someone else! You are not her boss, I am!"

It was perhaps the first time in a studio position where my boss had referred to me respectfully as "an artist."

With Felipe's encouragement after a year at this 6th Avenue fabric house, I left the 9 to 5 fashion industry studio position to start my own textile design company, Kim Parker Designs. That last studio job had given me great confidence when producing my own floral designs on fabric. I was ready to take flight on my own and see if I could sell my own original hand painted patterns to the fashion industry. I had no idea how I would go about doing it, no plan. But I knew that the designs I'd been creating for this fabric house for a year were selling well. This gave me enough impetus to kick free of the 9 to 5 studio painting jobs and start my own small print selling studio.

Kim Parker Designs

During the year that I painted at the last fabric house, I became friendly with a Turkish artist named Serif. He was a fellow Aquarian, a fine painter and also a gifted musician. We shared an equal enthusiasm for both art and music. He had earned a degree in design and possessed technical skills as a painter that I didn't have. After work, he would play his guitar and other lute-like Turkish stringed instruments at home. I was coming from the opposite direction, with a degree in music, while painting was my hobby and passion after work hours.

In his small studio apartment on East 37th Street we would joyfully compose flute and guitar compositions and record them. These improvisations were full of color, humor and texture. We had a natural musical dialogue together.

On his tiny apartment wall were large- scale paintings produced on substantial pieces of wood he had found and carted home from the New York City streets. He was wonderfully resourceful. Between Turkish cups of tea and tasty delights, we created quite a body of original musical compositions together. With Felipe, the three of us together, combed flea market lots on weekends for unique objects. Afterward, we would often cook each other delicious meals on our very tight budgets.

My plan to sell my own original designs to the fashion industry would be harder than I had anticipated. I contacted print companies- studios and agencies in the fashion industry that represented textile designers from around the world and sold their designs to fashion houses. Each one had their specific look, and time after time, my look just didn't fit in with their collections. Asked to paint teddy bears with balloons, or Hermes faux jewels and chains, I simply couldn't push my brushes in that way. My designs were all free - handed and painted in vivid colors of my own choosing. I was not interested in trends and my style was freer and more organic than what I was seeing in their portfolios.

After not having seen each other for about a year, Serif and I ran into one another on the city streets. He too was looking for work, was unemployed, and having no luck.

"I think you should meet with Designs NY in Soho," he said. "They sell prints to the fashion industry. I have a feeling the owner of this agency would really like your work."

Serif provided me with her contact information and in exchange for his kindness I invited him up for dinner.

The print studio in Soho was located in an impressive loft space on Broadway. Patty, Its owner, was a painter herself. She represented the work of many talented textile designers around the world, and was running a successful business in New York City. As Serif had predicted, she really liked my work. This company was highly respected and well established and sold many designs to the fashion industry.

When I opened my cases of hand painted prints to show her, she was instantly excited to join forces, suggesting that I learn to paint on silk.

"Your sales will double. Your work will look amazing on silk once you learn this technique," she said enthusiastically.

In just thirty minutes she demonstrated this new silk painting technique, a skill that allowed me to paint more directly onto the fabric's slick and glossy surface. This was an exciting artistic breakthrough moment for me as a textile designer. I was using a new medium that made my vivid color sense come to life like never before.

Now that I had learned this new painting technique, there were supplies I needed to have in order to produce a substantial amount of silk designs. I ran around the city purchasing them: everything from a large aluminum cylinder and lobster pot on the Lower East Side, to silk dyes and sponges, new brushes, wooden frames, tacks and gutta serti. Once I started painting on silk using this new technique, I simply could not stop. I was like the dancer in The Red Shoes.

The fabric's soft, floppy quality made them completely irresistible to the touch. Before I knew it, I was submitting hundreds of new floral and geometric designs to her for her silk collection to sell.

One afternoon, Lena, her salesgirl secretly confessed when we were alone:

"Kim, I just wanted you to know, your work really stands out from the rest of the designs I rep in print appointments. When I show them to my clients in the fashion industry, they really react positively to them."

This feedback was very important for me to hear. Lena was showing and selling literally thousands of textile designs every day to her fashion industry clients. I had little confidence that mine would be noticed amid so many beautiful works.

After a few months working for this Soho agency, Felipe said to me:

"Honey, what if you went out and sold your designs directly to the fashion industry yourself? What if you pulled in the entire profit on a design? I believe you can do it."

I always appreciated his positive support and belief in me, but I didn't have a single client to sell my designs to. I had no idea how in the world I would find even one client - let alone rep my own portfolio of work to an entire industry! How would I get my foot in the door in these fashion companies? No one knew who I was. I had no big studio name, no reputation, not a single connection.

After a few months of submitting silk designs to Patty at her Soho print studio, I mentioned to her that my "hope" going forward, was to create an entirely new body of designs separate from the ones in her possession and to earn more money. I would try to sell the new ones on my own to the fashion industry. I was not at all interested in competing with her business. How could I anyway? I knew no one. I was just one person with one look to offer. Her textile design studio had hundreds of artists from all over the world provided many different artistic looks to choose from, and she had a Rolodex of hundreds of faithful clients. I didn't even have one!

"Kim, I cannot accept this arrangement," Patty said. "You will be competing with me."

I was surprised by her reaction. It seemed obvious to me that this idea was clearly in her favor, not mine. She had been in the print selling business for many years. She had been running a very successful company with a long –standing good reputation. I knew not one single company or design director to contact. She told me that if this was the direction I was going to take, that she would hand me back my seven hundred designs. I was not instantly sure what I was going to do, but I took them home.

Now the challenge was all mine. How would I get companies like Gap, Old Navy, JCrew, Ann Taylor or anyone to buy a single design from me and take my little print-selling studio seriously? So with my heavy portfolio cases of seven hundred original hand painted prints, I set out to the garment industry's streets. I rolled my cases up and down Seventh Avenue, 8th Avenue and Broadway, entering all buildings, riding the elevators equipped with homemade business cards in hand, and hope in my heart.

I stopped on every single floor of each building, entering countless shiny showrooms where racks of clothes were hanging through glass doors, and politely introducing myself as Kim Parker Designs. My business card was left with anyone who would take one. Sometimes designers would ask to see a glimpse of what I was selling in my cases as a "preview." Others quickly indicated they never purchased original prints for their lines. Every fashion door was different.

There were no emails back then, so I made a million phone calls to follow up. Every night I continued to paint and expand my collection and body of work, without a single print appointment scheduled in my book. I continued to paint new floral and geometric prints daily, placing calls with a hope that someone would schedule an appointment with me to see my collection. Finally, I got my first print appointment in the fashion industry on Madison Avenue.

Intimate Exchange

My very first Kim Parker Designs print appointment in the fashion industry, was with a famous designer lingerie house on lower Madison Avenue. I remembered reading that this intimates company owner had been a concert violinist before she pursued a career in fashion design. I was inspired that we shared a background in classical music. I thought this might lead to something positive.

The Design Director, the company print buyer, had made the appointment with me. He was an older gentleman about seventy years of age. He had apparently worked there for many years. I remember rolling my print cases that first morning into the conference room, full of hope. I was also a bit nervous too about showing my original hand painted silk designs. It was my first day.

After ten minutes of displaying my work upon the conference room table, he remained silent. He stared almost in a daze at my designs but said nothing as I went through each motion of turning the white pages gently. Suddenly he put his hand firmly and aggressively over my print pile and said angrily, "I've had enough! Please put these away now! You can go!" My heart fell suddenly to my feet. His angry outburst brought tears instantly to my eyes. After weeks and weeks of preparation and hope, my efforts were met on my very first day, with an almost violent response.

I began carefully and quickly preparing my print cases to leave. I kept quiet as my eyes were quickly welling up with tears. Looking down, I took a deep breath while taking a moment to look more closely at the man sitting across the conference room table. He seemed withered, white haired and sad looking. I found myself saying:

"Do you mind me asking what astrological sign you are?"

He looked curiously at me and replied, "Aries, why?"

"Oh, nothing," I said, "I was just wondering. I am usually good at guessing people's astrological signs."

"What sign are you?" he asked me. "I am Aquarius," I said.

Suddenly his sad and angry expression changed, as if he was coming back to life.

"That's my favorite sign in the world," he said. "My partner, the love of my life of forty-five years, was Aquarius. Do you know that Aries and Aquarius are the most compatible signs? I lost my partner to AIDS a few years ago," he said.

"I am really sorry," I said gently.

For the next thirty minutes he openly shared a few of his precious memories about his beloved Aquarian companion. I sat across the table listening, and not moving a muscle. One simple astrological question had led to this incredible outpouring of grief, emotion and cherished memories. This was my very first print appointment in the fashion industry. I was amazed at the level of intimacy he shared with me, a perfect stranger. But it was not lost on me. I was grateful for this touching exchange. I soon put aside my own feelings of disappointment. I could see his humanity now, a man evidently still steeped in sorrow over the loss of a beloved partner.

Gathering my coat when he was finished, I got up to leave.

"Let me walk you to the door," he said.

I put my hand out to shake his, and he kissed it gently.

"Kim, I am sorry for the way I treated you earlier. You didn't deserve that. Your work is beautiful. You will do very well," he said. We hugged briefly and then I left.

When I got out onto Madison Avenue, I took a deep breath of cold November air. I wondered whether all print appointments going forward were going to be like that one. As I wheeled my cases back home that first day, I was not sure what to expect about this new chosen path. The brisk city walk down Madison Avenue helped release my own disappointment providing me with strength and renewal.

The very next day, in my second print appointment with another lingerie fashion company on Madison Avenue, I sold two silk designs right up the street. The Design Director said enthusiastically, "I have never seen such beautiful work in all my life." I swiftly realized that no two print appointments would ever be the same. I was now on my way to running my own print-selling business Kim Parker Designs, in New York City, where I suspected a greater spectrum of human color awaited me.

The King of the Fashion Industry

During that first year up and running Kim Parker Designs, I rolled my cases through the fashion industry's many heavy revolving doors on Broadway and Seventh Avenue, selling my prints to high-end fashion designers, dress and blouse companies, children's wear companies to fabric developers. It took time to get used to being face to face with design teams, showing my work to young teams of firing squads who openly either liked or disliked my collection, but in retrospect, it taught me to believe in my work, and become more of an observer than become entangled and searching for approval.

"Blouse- House Marvin," (a name I privately referred to a steady print-buying client of mine in the fashion industry) told me one afternoon about a colleague whom he referred to as: "The King of The Fashion Industry." "The King" apparently bought many prints from print selling studios. After I was given his contact information, I phoned him to see whether he would like to schedule an appointment with me. Blouse-House Marvin had described him as "a man at the very top of the fashion industry; a real veteran whose approval was met by few."

In truth, I was a bit nervous about meeting him. I was new to this print selling world. I wondered how a man who had seen *everything* would react to my collection of prints? Not long into our phone exchange he said gruffly, "I want you to know that I have seen it all. Unless you think you have something special, please don't waste my time, as I am incredibly busy."

I went to bed that night feeling very nervous about this upcoming print appointment the next morning. I worried that he would instantly reject my work. If he had seen *everything* there was to see? And what would be special about what I had to offer? The very next morning I rolled my portfolio cases up Seventh Avenue to his showroom.

The showroom was clean and contemporary with floor to ceiling mirrors and small café sized round tables with chairs. Suddenly a wide width, tall man with greasy black hair thinly draped across his large balding head greeted me. He was speaking loudly into one of those heavy-duty old portable phones the size of a shoe – kind of like Maxwell Smart. While he was engaged in a conversation on the phone, he manually directed me to set myself up on one of the small, round café tables.

These little round tables in the showroom were not large enough to sip coffee on. There was definitely not enough surface area to accommodate my rectangular large cases of prints. The only way for me to display my collection of designs for him would have been to acrobatically bend one of my legs to the height of the café table, lean half the case across my thigh, and manually, on one foot go through the usual motion of displaying hundreds of pages that were stacked inside the case, a real balancing act.

But willingly of course, I became a Cirque de Soleil contortionist. Mark didn't seem to mind the effort it involved. I displayed my collection while he continued speaking on the shoe phone. "Joe, I have to get off the phone now," he suddenly said, "I have a print studio here in front of me. I think I'm in the presence of a genius."

Turning to me with a smile he said, "So how come you didn't tell me on the phone yesterday that you were a genius?" Pulling many designs aside with great enthusiasm one after the other, I couldn't believe how well things were going.

"We are a very successful California dress company, you know. We do a very large print business here on silk. We will probably wind up buying most of the designs I have pulled today from your line. Can you please keep these designs aside for me until tomorrow morning?" he asked, "The President of the company is coming in on the Red Eye from LA. I want her to see all of them before we go ahead and purchase them."

I quickly did the math. This could have turned out to be a very lucrative appointment and new client, so naturally I agreed to return the next morning with all of the designs he was interested in.

The very next morning I arrived at his showroom at 9:00a.m. The King of Fashion was in the president's office behind glass doors. I waited about a half hour on a bench in the foyer before he called me to come in and display my textile design collection.

The conference table in the president's office was as long as a bowling alley. In the middle of this long, shiny surface, I opened my portfolio case, setting the healthy stack of designs on the table. The president of the company was a woman in her early sixties wearing an expensive looking Chanel suit. She had just flown in on the red eye from LA. From across the room while on her phone, she signaled me to begin displaying my prints upon her table. This perplexed me, as she was quite a distance away from me. I didn't really have her full attention. Thirty seconds into showing her the prints that were pulled aside, she mouthed, "Thanks very much. These are not for us." And just like that, hopes were quickly dashed.

A cold sweat of disappointment coursed through me. I packed my cases and slipped out the door as fast as possible. Even though I was disappointed, I knew it was an important experience. From that moment on I learned not to have expectations, and more importantly, never to feel intimidated by someone described to me as "The King of Fashion," (No one could hold such a title except Paul Poiret after all!).

"My Little Victoria's Secret"

One evening, after a very long and tiring day of print selling appointments, close to dinnertime, the phone rang. "This is Victoria's Secret calling for Kim Parker Designs. We are looking for summer floral prints and we were told you had some beautiful designs." I had actually never sold any of my designs to Victoria's Secret. Other industry print studios mentioned that they were one of their best clients, often purchasing designs in bundles for their ladies' lingerie and swimwear collections.

At 5:00pm I jumped into a cab, heading up 6th Avenue to the corner of 42nd Street to the W.R. Grace building. I remember being in that building before when temping as a secretary in my mid-twenties at HBO. The audible, loud clicking of high heels upon that shiny, marble, lobby floor was the first thing I noticed.

The elevator moved swiftly and smoothly to the Victoria's Secret office. The view of The New York Public Library and Bryant Park at night was spectacular. I was greeted by the receptionist who pointed me in the direction of their conference room at the end of the hallway. "You can set your cases up in there. We will be in shortly," she said. The conference room was brightly lit, and I knew right away that my hand painted silk prints would really sparkle like jewels under those lights.

The head designer for Victoria's Secret entered the conference room. She had a very kind face. "Sorry for calling you here at this late hour on such short notice. I was told you had some really beautiful floral designs," she said warmly. "I'm really only interested in seeing what you have on silk, not paper. Most of what we will be producing will be for our silk lingerie line." I took her carefully through the many pages of my silk portfolio. She instantly started pulling floral designs aside. Once finished pulling prints, we went through the editing process, narrowing her selection down to a mere forty.

Of course this type of purchase potential, the possibility of selling such a large quantity of my designs, especially at the end of the workday, was a very exciting prospect, and most unusual. "I will need to show them to my boss before we make a decision," she told me. "Can I take this pile of prints with me into the other room while you wait here?" she asked.

Typically, this kind of request to remove designs from a room was *not* really OK. Color copying an original piece of artwork was something a number of industry companies did when they couldn't afford to buy an original design. Showing them to their resident artist who was sitting in the design studio (who could then go and knock them off) was not atypical.

I knew Victoria's Secret had a big enough budget to purchase original artwork. I was just a small business operating by myself, not a large print-selling studio in New York City representing hundreds of textile artists. "Could you please ask your boss whether she'd mind coming into the conference room instead to see them? We can spread the designs out over the table for her here," I said. I could see from her facial expression that she was not used to such a request. I imagined that most print studios simply obliged because they saw the earning potential. Usually sales reps were not especially protective of the artwork since it wasn't their own personal intellectual property, as it was mine.

She left the room to go and get her boss. It was now nearing 7:00pm. There were forty designs perfectly laid out across the surface of the table for her boss to see. Ten minutes later he boss entered the conference room. She seemed pleased with what we had pulled aside.

After further editing the selection, twenty designs now remained on the table. "OK, here's what we want to do going forward," she said. "We're VERY interested in these twenty designs of yours. Most likely we will buy most of them from you, but we need to borrow them for our meeting early tomorrow morning. Instead of you coming back with them in the morning, can we keep them here overnight and just call you after our meeting is finished? You can come by then and pick them up."

One side of my brain was saying, "They will just be in their possession overnight, Kim. Just let them hold onto them. This could be a big sale, and a very important new client." But I found myself saying, "I wish I could do that, but I am just a small print studio here in New York. I have an early print appointment tomorrow morning and not having these twenty designs in my portfolio could mean I'd be losing out on a potential sale. I hope you understand. This is just my company policy, since I am just a small studio."

Looking somewhat uneasy at first, she left the room for another ten minutes. I was sure she was going to return to tell me to pack up my cases; that they were not interested in the designs they'd pulled aside any longer. I knew they had many other print studios too they were meeting with in New York. Those studios would willingly have left hundreds of original designs overnight in their possession.

When she returned to the showroom she said, "Can you please write these prints up for me? We'll purchase them all." I wasn't sure I was hearing this correctly. "*All* of them?" I asked. "Yes, all." she said. "I will need to sign the invoice once you've written them up, so let's try to wrap things up quickly, so we can all go home, as it is late." I took a deep breath. Sitting at the conference room table, I carefully listed each one by name and number on my company invoice, and handed it to her for signature.

That cold evening in the dark while rolling my print cases home along 6th Avenue past Bryant Park and The New York Public Library, to our loft apartment on Broadway and West 31st Street, I felt high as a kite. In the face of a fashion industry giant used to making their own rules, my little print company stood by its principles, and at Victoria's Secret, I was "victorious."

Meeting Liena

Kathy, a dress client on Broadway bought a silk floral print from me one afternoon. She was a very pretty Irish girl, young and vibrant in energy. I instantly guessed her astrological sign, Gemini. The hand painted silk print she had purchased for her dress line a month before was one of my personal favorites.

"Kim, I am calling because the other day when I brought your silk design to a converter here in New York to be developed into fabric, the company President, Nigel, asked me where I had purchased it. He said he had been waiting years to see a design of this caliber. I hope you don't mind? I gave him your name and contact information. He is British and has his own fabric company. It's a family run business," she said.

She told me that Nigel had asked that I give him a call to set up a print appointment, so I did just that.

Nigel was a tall, grey- tufted man in his late sixties. When I arrived at his Broadway address, it looked more like a corporate office than the typical fashion showroom. I opened my cases up along his windowsill ledge instead of a conference room table, the only available, flat surface for displaying. Nigel was quiet at first. I was not sure what to make of his silence while I went through my usual motions of displaying my case of prints. Kathy had told me of his very excited reaction to the silk design she had purchased from me saying, "I have been waiting to see designs of this caliber! Where did you buy it?"

After I finished my presentation, Nigel asked,

"Are you familiar with the painter Sonia Delaunay?"

"Yes, I am," I said, "I have always loved her work."

"Well you should know that we have the largest archive of her original hand painted textiles on fabrics," he said proudly. "My family have been in the fabric business for decades. We have a massive archive of her original work."

He then showed me an old heavy, dusty binder with pages of wonderful fabric swatches mounted inside, most of which were Sonia Delaunay's textile prints produced on old quality linens and cotton. They all had a very vintage and charmingly dated appeal. They belonged in a museum.

He said nothing about my work though as I went through the motions of showing him my hundreds of my hand painted silk prints.

"How would you like to meet the great designer, Liena?," he suddenly asked.

I had been a fan of her gorgeous Bohemian fashions for years. By this time, I had already sold my original textile designs to many of her fashion colleagues, such as Diane Von Furstenburg, Jill Stuart, Carolina Herrera, to name a few. Liena's bohemian style clothes were extremely appealing to my own fashion sense. She was one of the few high- end designers I had yet to meet, so of course the prospect of finally meeting her, excited me.

"I love her work. I would very much like the chance to meet her," I said.

"Well, this is what I want you to do for *me*. Go home and paint about ten new silk designs that look similar to the work of Sonia Delaunay. I don't want floral designs. They have to be geometric and look just like hers. I will take them to show her in my next fabric appointment and see whether she has any interest in using them."

I wondered why I needed to paint like Sonia Delaunay when I had two cases of hundreds of original designs of my own? I wondered why he had showed such unbridled enthusiasm for one of my floral silk designs to Kathy, but in our print appointment showed little to no interest or enthusiasm? Why was it necessary to paint like a modern day Sonia Delaunay?

In those early days however, I bent and flexed to everyone's requests. I viewed everything as an opportunity to grow. Jones New York's formal dress division had once requested I paint a large Georgia O'Keefe–like floral for a silk evening gown. I honestly never thought I could do it, but I did. The floral print turned out beautifully once developed into a garment.

After my meeting with Nigel, I went home and painted some silk prints a la Sonia Delaunay. A week later I phoned him to let him know that I had new designs to show him as per his request. Shortly thereafter, we met at his office on Broadway with my cases and we wheeled over to Liena's 8th Avenue design studio.

I wanted to wear something pretty that day when meeting her. I decided on a jade green paisley sundress that had a definite Bohemian style with some strappy summer sandals. On the way there Nigel said to me,

"When we get to her studio, you will sit by the front door until I signal you to join us. I will be showing her my own archive of original Sonia Delaunay prints. I know she's going to love them. We may not even get an opportunity to show her the prints you painted for the meeting," he said.

When we arrived, the elevator doors opened right up into Liena's studio directly. Racks of beautiful printed dresses could be spotted in the distance along the back window. A white cafeteria-like table stood a few feet away from the entrance for print displaying. Her workspace was as I had imagined it might be, eclectic and Bohemian.

Nigel came fully equipped to show his own family archive of original Sonia Delaunay vintage swatches that to my eyes looked a bit out-dated even though they were totally collector's items. They were beautiful in an old world, charming sort of way but their colors looked washed out and even drab by modern day printing standards.

As instructed, I sat in the front, in a dark corner silently by the elevator doors. Nigel spent about thirty minutes pulling his Delaunay swatches from his own cases to show Liena. Then I saw her pointing at me.

"Whom did you bring with you?" she asked.

"Oh, she's just a small print studio," Nigel said dismissively.

"Can I see her collection too?" Liena asked.

Somewhat annoyed I suppose due to Liena's lack of interest for Nigel's Sonia Delaunay collection, he asked me to come over in an unfriendly tone and manner. I greeted Liena, shaking her hand at the table and smiling. I had always been such a huge fan of her beautiful fashions. I had browsed the racks of her Soho store for decades wishing I could afford most of what was on the rack but they were too expensive for me.

As I opened up my cases on the table, Nigel said,

'"Now *just* show us the Sonia Delaunay prints I asked you to bring along for this meeting that are on top."

Liena said nothing as I went through the motions of showing her the new geometric prints I had painted a la Sonia Delaunay. But when we got to my original hand painted floral designs directly underneath, she started fervently pulling my floral prints aside and with great enthusiasm said,

"These are so beautiful! Please pull this one out and that one for me as well."

Finally there were many designs on the table in front of her, all of which were silk and floral in pattern, not geometric. I remember one in particular being a print I didn't want to sell to anyone because I loved it so much. After editing her final selection she said,

"By the way Kim, I love your dress! Where did you get it?"

With a smile, I couldn't resist admitting, "I got it at TJ Maxx and it was only fifteen dollars!"

"Great find!" she said with a knowing smile. Nigel was very quiet throughout our girlish exchange. He drew up an invoice for the designs she wanted to purchase from me. Soon we said our goodbyes.

In the elevator however, as soon as the door shut, Nigel turned angrily to me. With a beet red face he said,

"How dare you tell a great designer like Liena, that you bought your dress for fifteen dollars at TJ Maxx! How utterly distasteful!"

I remained quiet inside the elevator until we got to the ground floor. I knew Liena liked my dress. I had seen her many weekends for years and years shopping the fashion vendors at the local Chelsea flea market parking lot purchasing antique clothes for her vintage–inspired collections, just as many New York designers did.

But Nigel kept his haughty composure while we rode the elevator together to the main floor. I think what was perhaps "utterly distasteful" to him was Liena's unexpected enthusiasm for my floral designs, and not his archival Sonia Delaunay geometric prints. He could not show an ounce of delight over the sale. He would now be required to put my floral prints into fabric development for her.

The prints she had bought from my collection wound up in her runway shows and on the racks of her stores, in beautiful dresses and blouses produced in the finest fabrics. I was invited to attend her fashion shows in Bryant Park where I could see my floral designs showcased in her collections. A part of me wished I could have some of the fabric to make something special, but it was clear to me that Nigel and I would never speak again. I didn't know Liena well enough to ask her for a yard of fabric.

However, just two years later, another print client of mine told me about a store called Mood Fabrics in the garment industry. This was long before Mood Fabrics had become the ever-popular designer fabric remnant house it is today, popularized by the TV show *Project Runway*. I went there just looking for some velvet one afternoon, and much to my incredible surprise and delight, I came upon three huge bolts of this favorite floral design of mine on that wonderful cotton lawn fabric, the one I loved most that Liena had purchased from me. I had created two color versions of that particular floral design as per her request, and both of them were there on full display in generous sized amounts for purchase. I bought all three bolts for a very reasonable price, and proudly carted them home.

A Striped Past

I love the following story because it has the magic of an O'Henry tale. Adrianna Papel, the fashion designer who dresses Vanna White on *Wheel of Fortune*, was the very first fashion studio painting position I had ever held. Six years later in 2001, before we finally launched the Kim Parker ® brand, I worked in many such studios in the fashion industry. Finally, I left that painting 9 to 5 existence behind, and went out on my own to sell my original textile designs to many of these fashion houses independently. To my memory, the Adrianna Papel art studio was full of gifted FIT and Parsons graduates all possessing technical skills I had never learned.

On high studio shelves to the ceiling there were small jars of plastic paint cups, each carefully labeled with Nippon numbers written on them. There could be fifty shades of jade green, sixty variations of magenta, or forty shades of plum, each color different by just a tiny degree. Nippon was the name of a precise color system established by the fashion industry to help identify and indicate to overseas factories exactly which color to use when printing a garment.

Angelika, my Greek thirty-something year old boss and head of the studio, was an attractive woman. She was stylish and chic with dark brown hair and big beautiful eyes. She would come through the studio door tossing her fur capes and expensive scarves each morning over available studio chairs. She flashed her rather sizable diamond ring when joyfully announcing her engagement. Always scented in fine perfume, everyone could see that she had gone to great lengths each day to put herself together stylishly. Admittedly, she was beautiful.

Every morning Angelika left me instructions on my drafting table indicating which number Nippon bottles to pull off the high shelves and begin using on an assigned design. There were many art supplies in the studio too that were unfamiliar to me, one of which was a ruling pen.

A ruling pen was used for cleanly rendering an "engineered stripe." (I still don't know how to use one to this day!) I was given an Hermes print to copy and repaint, a gaudy design with sparkling faux jewels and ribbons in jade greens and hot magentas, a repeated palette Adrianna Papel's clients were accustomed to seeing in the majority of her clothes.

Angelika knew when she hired me that I didn't have the technical skills the FIT and Parsons students had all possessed. I was hired yet again, based purely upon a small book of hand painted designs that I had created. My resume at that time showed no design experience whatsoever, just a degree in Flute Performance from Oberlin College Conservatory of Music.

She knew I was coming to her with my own small book of hand painted designs and nothing more. In my interview she seemed pleased with them. However, once employed and in the studio, my freehanded approach was of no use. I was not able to paint my own versions of flowers or geometric designs. I was expected to render and reproduce very technically precise motifs and prints to "note perfection." There was no room for error or sloppiness. Anything I was learning technically, I had to learn on the job, right in front of people like Angelika.

I sometimes chuckle a bit when I replay the exchanges we had during those first three months of employment.

"How did you paint this stripe design, Kim?" she asked one morning (while looking cattily over my shoulder at the other artists in the room in disbelief.) The real question being asked was,

"Do you really think this stripe you just painted is good enough for *my* studio?" Innocently I replied,

"What do you mean *how* did I paint it Angelika? I painted it with a paintbrush of course." A giggle escaped a few of my fellow designers in the room. Angelika turned red.

"Come into my office," she said sternly.

"How can I keep you here when you don't know what a ruling pen is? Or how to use one?" she asked. "All of our stripes are rendered with a ruling pen, not by hand. I showed your stripe to Paul in our sales department, and he asked me how I could keep you in my design studio? He thinks I should fire you," she told me.

I replied, "Angelika, you hired me based upon my small book of hand painted designs. You knew that I had not graduated from FIT or Parsons. I have a degree in Flute Performance from Oberlin College Conservatory of Music as is clearly stated on my resume. If you are unhappy with me, I am sorry. I am trying my best, really I am."

Angelika took a deep breath. She looked somewhat exasperated. "I will give you one more chance," she said. "Try to go home and learn how to use a ruling pen tonight."

That night I took home a ruling pen and sat at my kitchen table for hours trying to master this little tool. Mae, my Korean friend in the studio who could paint anything and everything under the sun with great technical precision showed me how to use one when we were alone in the studio.

"It took me two years in school to master this tool, and learn how to paint a stripe cleanly with it. It's not an easy technique to learn in one night. Good luck, Kim," she said kindly. I was fired two weeks later.

Six whole years after, however, when running my own print-selling studio, Kim Parker Designs, I bravely decided to return to the scene of this crime. I called Adrianna Papel to see whether they might like to schedule a print appointment and see my print collection.

When I arrived at this Seventh Avenue showroom, everything looked smaller to me than I had remembered six years back when first starting out. It was my first studio job in the fashion industry, and no doubt, everything looked more intimidating to me then.

I was surprised to see that Paul, the sales manager who wanted Angelika to fire me because I was unable to neatly render an engineered stripe with a ruling pen, was still working there six years later. Paul didn't remember me. Angelika, however, had been long gone. And like a perfect ending to an O'Henry tale, he purchased one of my hand painted stripe designs from my silk print collection, and said,

"You know, your stripes in particular are really beautiful."

It's a Wrap

In a West Village design studio, a favorite destination for a print appointment, I met the iconic creator of the wrap dress. Her showroom was not located (like all other fashion houses were) in the garment district on 7th Avenue. Her office was located on a beautiful, quiet, cobblestone street in the old meat-packing district, which had not yet become the very trendy fashion zip code it is today.

Back then it was a quieter neighborhood along the Hudson River surrounded by old New York City culinary institutions like *Florent*, the trendy French diner that sadly closed its doors in 2008. The surrounding area was actually mostly full of smelly meat markets with blood running in the gutters and large beef carcasses visibly hanging on meat hooks inside open-faced warehouses. By night, prostitutes and drag queens frequented those old cobblestone streets. There were a few fine art galleries too along 14th Street.

Her design studio was a beautiful oasis, surrounded by a very cutting edge New York City scene that no longer exists. Nowadays, these same streets are lined with fashion boutiques, cafes, and the brilliant new Whitney Museum and the beloved Highline.

Catherine (who at that time was the head designer there, years before she launched her own highly successful namesake brand) called me to schedule a print appointment specifically requesting that I "bring only my silk designs" to this print appointment.

What I loved about entering this West Village showroom was that the space was full of life, New York Pop culture and color. Paintings of her created by Andy Warhol graced the lobby. There was a lovely fountain, centrally located, with mosaic tiling. There was a spiral staircase that led to offices a floor above where the designers sat at their stations.

I was pleasantly escorted to a table off the lobby and asked to set myself up for a team of her designers to sit in on my appointment. Ten minutes into my silk print presentation, this famous wrap dress icon made her appearance. Looking over my shoulder while I was displaying my designs, She asked:

"What studio is this?"

"Kim Parker Designs," Catherine replied.

"Have we ever bought from this studio before?" she asked.

"Yes we have. In fact, we currently have a few of Kim's floral prints in our spring collection," Catherine replied.

"Are these *your* silk designs, Kim? Did you paint these all yourself?" she asked.

"Yes, I did," I replied.

Continuing to watch the print presentation, and pulling several of my original silk floral textile designs aside she said:

"Catherine, please purchase a few of these for spring."

Towards the end of the appointment, she asked Catherine which of my prints were currently in her collection. Moments later she disappeared into a back room, and returned carrying a beautiful pink floral skirt in her hands.

"Kim, this is for you, and I hope it's your size," this icon said smiling. I instantly thanked her for it. The skirt with my design on it was beautiful and so stylish.

"You are very talented," she said warmly, and then walked away.

It was certainly a memorable print appointment. The floral skirt she gave me with my pink and black floral design on it fit me perfectly and I wore it proudly for many years to come.

Jill loves Pink Too

J ill was one of my favorite fashion designers. Her clothes were mostly vintage –inspired, and made with sumptuous silks and velvets. I came upon her designer showroom purely by accident one afternoon when looking for new print clients in buildings along Seventh Avenue.

Getting off the elevator on her floor, I was drawn instantly into a showroom that was full of the most beautiful, princess-like dresses, skirts and blouses. I felt as if I was entering a dream. Every rack of velvet dresses and skirts, organza blouses adorned in the finest embroidery sparkled like jewels to my eyes. The receptionist in the showroom allowed me to wait there with my print cases introducing me to one of her young designers.

"Can you show me some of your prints now?" he asked smiling.

Directing me to the showroom table, I set myself up never imagining that it would turn into a full-blown print appointment the way it had. After five minutes the young designer asked,

"I don't mean to be rude, but could you just wait here? I am going to get Jill. She must see these!"

Jill entered the showroom. I felt an instant connection to her on an aesthetic level. This was the first time that I had ever felt total aesthetic kinship with another line in the fashion industry. Every single skirt and blouse in her showroom had the kind of classic elegance and uniquely beautiful, costume, Ballet Russes kind of *contessa* type of beauty that I loved. We soon discovered we shared a mutual affection for the color pink. Her line had rose- colored embroidered velvet skirts and blouses with Juliette –like billowing sleeves. Everything on those racks cast their magic spells upon me. I wanted to wear every single garment.

Jill started enthusiastically pulling my silk designs aside on the table while I was presenting them. Before I knew it she had purchased a good many. We had an immediate appreciation for each other's gifts.

"Whenever you have new designs, "she said, "Please call me right away and just come in!"

And for a few years, we shared a truly inspired collaboration. My designs were printed on the finest silks and cottons. She kindly gave me a discount card to her Soho store that was like a costume museum to me. She generously gave me dresses and blouses with my own floral prints on them, and invited me to attend her fashion shows in Bryant Park where they were showcased on the runway. Soon after, a blouse with one of my floral designs was featured on the cover of WWD (Women's Wear Daily), in Bazaar Magazine and then, appeared in the movie "The Princess Diaries."

To this day I have held onto her beautiful dresses, blouses and skirts with my floral designs on them. They are simply gorgeous, timeless pieces. It was a sweet *pas de deux* for a few years; and my floral prints were featured in her designer collections for a few seasons.

Wisdom in a Schmatta House

Many of the fashion print selling appointments that I had during those six years were far from glamorous. One freezing rainy day in January, waiting with two 70 lbs print cases to hail a cab on the corner of 31st Street and Broadway, I managed miraculously to arrive at my print appointment on time. I was meeting with a woman's dress company I had never sold to before.

I could tell instantly upon arrival that we were not on the same page aesthetically. There were racks of "schmattas" (rags) in a sea of drab beige, grey and brown mixed with cheaply printed polyester animal prints.

The print buyer entered the reception area.

"You'll have to sit for another hour, sorry… I'm running late… unless you'd prefer to reschedule?" she asked.

Semi-drenched and having paid a handsome taxi fare to get there, I decided to wait. After an hour she returned, directing me into a darkly lit showroom.

"I'm again sorry for the condition of the room, but you'll have to display your collection on the floor," she said. "Our conference room table, as you can see, is full of boxes and I don't have enough time to remove them."

Hunched over my portfolio on my knees in a very awkward position and uncomfortable, I put my cases down on the dirty, linoleum floor to display my print collection, going through hundreds of my silk designs. Throughout the presentation she was completely silent. Finally she stopped me at a particular leaf print I had painted. It was a print I had always disliked. I had often thought about pulling it from my collection. The colors were sad and lifeless and all of my other designs were richly colorful. The print was extremely drab looking. She took it in her hands and looked long and hard at it for a few minutes.

"Ok, you can put it back, I don't want it," she said.

By the end of this forty-five minute session upon the floor, my back and neck were hurting from kneeling on my knees over the hard surface.

"Your look is not good for us," she said. (These were words that I instantly processed as a compliment.)

"Please try to pull your cases together as quickly as possible now. I have another studio appointment lined up right behind yours," she said.

I did my best to organize my delicate work as quickly as I could. Anyone who knows anything about handling silk designs knows that if you don't carefully put them back into your case, you will be spending hours later that evening ironing all of them.

While hustling to move myself out of there, she added in an unfriendly tone,

"You really should have more blue designs in your collection. I would have liked to have seen more blue prints, and less red and pink."

She was not incorrect that the majority of my prints were painted in warmer hues. I was never a huge fan of blue. I thanked her for the suggestion. Getting to my feet, I shook her hand, and made my way towards the door.

"Wait a minute!" she said suddenly. "I think I might want to see that leaf design again, can you find it fast? I would like to take another look at it."

Back on my knees and reopening my cases, I searched through hundreds of pages of silk designs in record time to locate it. When I finally found it, she examined it closely again for a few minutes while I remained quietly hunched over my portfolio on the floor.

"I'll take it," she said, "Please write up the invoice as quickly as possible."

I never could forget that print appointment, maybe mainly because of the ugly aesthetic aspect of it. But I remember keeping my balance and poise from start to finish while on my knees. From the outset it certainly seemed unlikely that I would make a sale, given the Grand Canyon of aesthetic difference between us.

However, I went home that night with her words in my head and I painted a few blue floral designs to add into my existing collection. And the very next day, the blue ones sold to another industry fashion house.

A Spacious Loft in Herald Square

Felipe and I moved to a 1700 sf loft space at 1234 Broadway and 31st Street, a stone's throw from Macy's at Herald Square. The apartment had 15- foot high ceilings and old wooden floors, fireplace and tall windows overlooking Broadway. The neighborhood is aptly called Koreatown. The building itself was an old Victorian, former single occupancy hotel once frequented by Al Capone and Bugsy Malone. The entire first floor of this old Victorian landmark building had been gut renovated and turned into mini loft apartments. All the above floors, (minus the penthouse), were occupied by Korean immigrants, a "flop house" basically, where entire Korean families were sadly stuffed like sardines into single rooms on bunk beds sharing one communal bathroom in the hallway. It was completely surreal.

The building was in truth very creepy. We moved to this edgy zip code because my print business had taken off. I needed to be closer to the fashion industry so I could handle the demand for print appointments more easily. I could roll my cases to most of my print appointments on foot and not by taxi.

Prior to living in that spooky Victorian building, we lived in a beautiful Gramercy Park Prewar, rent-stabilized apartment. The Russian

Revolutionary, Leon Trotsky, had once apparently occupied our particular apartment we were told. Unfortunately, we let go of that one bedroom rent-stabilized apartment when a neighbor's behavior became intolerable.

Moving into a larger, open loft space, sacrificing a beautiful neighborhood and low rent for an easier commute to the fashion industry was the trade-off. Our new neighborhood didn't even provide a tree within blocks. It was ugly and grey and industrial. Our front windows were filthy and dimmed by bus fumes on Broadway. The tenants in this Victorian landmark building reminded me of the odd figures one sees in an Ensor painting.

Wheeling my cases through those whistling narrow hallways to the elevator every morning, in retrospect, took courage. Some of the rodents in the building were the size of house cats. At night you could hear them scampering and squeaking in the ceiling right above our heads with their offspring. It was right out of the B-movie *Ben*. The loft was a gracious 1800 square feet with original teak wooden floors, and Victorian fixtures. The exposed brick fireplace added a degree of old world charm.

Two years into living in this spacious loft, Australian Vogue Living Magazine contacted me requesting an interview, sending their UK photographer to photograph our home interior. It was our first major designer profile in Vogue, when launching the Kim Parker brand.

I was able to paint my proudest body of work on both canvas as well as textile designs in this creepy building. I think it's a testament to human nature that when we lack something in our lives (in this case, greenery and a pretty city street) we instinctively find a way to create it for ourselves. Painted canvas gardens were pouring out of me in those days. I was producing a thousand textile designs a year for my print line.

I was able to expand and open creative gestures in a way I had not been able to before due to the larger square footage.

Felipe and I would jump into our old Chevy station wagon with golden retriever Maggie, picnicking in Central Park on the open lawn on my days off. During those three years in that former Victorian single occupancy hotel in that commercial zone, my print sales soared and tripled in the fashion industry. Appointments were rolling in. The amount of work on my end was incredible, in retrospect, selling prints by day and then painting them for hours at night.

Felipe decided to quit his job on Wall Street to help me manage my growing textile design company that he could see was a lot for one person to handle. After three years of loft living on Broadway in a filthy neighborhood, we were eager to return to our old elegant Gramercy Park zip code, which after three years we thankfully, finally did. We were so appreciative of the blossoming cherry trees on our block, and the Henry James-like charms of our landmark brownstone street.

Our new Gramercy Park apartment would soon become the perfect platform for the next fifteen years, an enchanted chapter in my design life. Our new home interior would be profiled on the Fine Living Network on TV and featured in countless international fashion and lifestyle publications such as ELLE, Living etc., YOU, PAGE SIX, The London Guardian, Country Living, ELLE Decoration UK and led to the publication of *Kim Parker Home: A Life in Design*, a critically acclaimed lifestyle coffee table book published by Harry N. Abrams in 2008.

Liz Claiborne and the Launch of a Brand

After more than five years of ghost designing and seeing my original textile designs appearing in the collections of top fashion and home furnishing brands such as Calvin Klein, DVF, Anna Sui, Jill Stuart, GAP, Anthropologie, Crate & Barrel and Pottery Barn, Felipe felt it was time to move in the direction of licensing and launch my namesake brand.

We launched our brand at the 2001 Licensing Show at the Jacob Javitz Center. Our booth was decorated with everything from hand painted designs mounted on posters -sized displays, to an upholstered vintage chair covered in my own floral fabric. I hand painted bowls and dishes in vibrant floral patterns for potential tabletop collaborations and mocked up floral note cards and stationery.

Companies such as: Lenox China, Block China, high -end rug companies, wall art companies, stationery manufacturers, and a gallery in the Hamptons, visited our booth, enthusiastically leaving their business cards behind. Follow up after the show was key.

What most people don't know about the licensing industry is that developing a product line with a manufacturer, whether bedding, bath, designer rugs, tableware, etc. takes *at least* a year and a half to create product before it hits the retail shelves. I was used to instant gratification during the years I sold my prints as a ghost designer. A "co-branded" partnership (ie: "Kim Parker for The Rug Company") now required familiarizing oneself with new contractual terms, royalties, and an understanding of the product's quality and the manufacturer's marketing efforts. A good attorney is needed to ensure that the contract is fair and protects the rights of the designer. There was a lot to learn when launching my brand.

No longer selling my prints to a majority of my fashion clients at this particular juncture, I only took print fashion appointments with certain clients as we transitioned to having a brand. We still had a Manhattan rent to pay. With the development of every new product on the market, our new licensing partners expected us to protect "the look" of our brand. This meant I couldn't sell that same look to competitors. Each product category involved lots of money invested by that company, time in manufacturing, promotion and selling of the collection. So towards the end of my print selling days in the fashion industry, while gradually phasing out print appointments, I had to be very mindful about not selling my designs to companies that would produce similar products with my signature style on them.

During that final print selling year, I remember a small, sweet victory though at the finish line. Liz Claiborne is one of the leaders of the fashion industry on Seventh Avenue. I rolled my design cases through their doors and into their showrooms twenty-seven times over the course of six years, always coming out empty-handed. Their office space on Broadway and 40th Street was modern and bright, with a boutique hotel-type of waiting area full of international fashion publications to read.

The designers were all always quite pleasant, often taking more than an hour to decide on whether a particular design would "work" for them. The refrain of, "Sorry, maybe next time. These are beautiful but this time, none of these worked for us" became all-too familiar. But typical of me, this didn't matter.

Having now however, a lot of work on the licensing side with the launch of my namesake brand, I didn't have the same free time to take these last print appointments as I had done always. Felipe took over in that last year, rolling my seventy-pound print cases through the industry streets, relieving me of these final appointments.

One afternoon Liz Claiborne called to schedule an appointment. I told Felipe that I had been there twenty-seven times in the course of six years. Later that afternoon when he returned home, he said,

"Guess what? I just sold ten prints to Liz Claiborne."

"You're kidding, right?" I said laughing.

"No, I am not," he said smiling. "I told the head designer that this was going to be her last print appointment with Kim Parker Designs. I mentioned to her that we were launching your new bedding and bath collections at Bloomingdale's next month. She looked at the designs as if they were precious jewels, and purchased ten of them. She then said,

"Please make sure to wish Kim my very best in the launch of her brand."

The Writing on the Wallpaper

Not long after the licensing show ended, we met with a number of companies to discuss potential designer collaborations for our brand. One meeting was with one of the top fabric and wallpaper companies in the US. They represented a number of the industry's leading designers and had showrooms all over the world. They also had an impressive space in the Design & Decorating Building in New York City.

The very first meeting was full of mutual enthusiasm. I arrived with my cases full of silk and paper prints displaying them over a large conference room table in their 5th Avenue showroom. The President and Design Director of the company were there, pulling aside designs on both hand painted linen and silk that we all felt would work best for both a couture and hospitality fabric and wallpaper collection under my brand name. They spoke of their many connections to large hotel chains in the US, and with showrooms worldwide.

The next nine months we worked on putting the designs into repeat and numerous color ways, scaling the prints up and down for both wallpapers and fabrics. Throughout these nine, long months we met a few times just to make sure things were developing smoothly. During that time, our attorneys were still hammering out all of the important contractual terms. It was a multi-million dollar designer program.

However, with each new meeting the communication seemed to grow more uncomfortable and negative in tone and I would often feel emotionally sickened, and unsettled. Despite a voice in my head telling me that this was a Red Flag, not a good sign at the start, I continued working on all of the design development for both the hospitality and couture collections. The President told us that early presentations of my collections were already of interest to a major hotel chain and that it could translate to a very substantial amount of money in all of our pockets.

Throughout those nine months of creating these collections, our attorney continued tightening the language of the contract and working through the terms with their lawyer. There were important protective clauses that needed to be added to the existing template. Finally, after nine whole months, the contract was ready to be signed and delivered.

At that time, the Fedex envelope arrived at our brownstone apartment with the two copies of the contract inside awaiting my signature. I sat quietly on our living room sofa staring at it. My stomach was in knots.

"Felipe, I am sorry, honey," I said suddenly, "I cannot sign this contract. It feels like we are entering into an abusive marriage for the next five years. It just doesn't feel right."

Felipe knew exactly how I felt. He had witnessed in numerous meetings the abusive behavior that was hard to ignore.

"Don't worry, honey," he said, "I will call our attorney. I'll just tell him the deal is off."

And an hour later, a nine–month long designing process vanished into thin air. I felt an instant sense of deep relief, much like I did when my ex-husband had finally moved out.

Felipe went over to the refrigerator and pulled out a bottle of wine that had been sitting in there for a year. "Honey, I have to tell you," he said chuckling, "you're one in a million. None of your designer colleagues in this industry would have ever had the courage to walk away from such a lucrative deal. The whole thing was totally Faustian, and honestly, I am proud of you for not selling your soul," he said.

It took many more years of meetings with wallpaper and fabric companies both in the US and UK before we finally signed on with the right licensing partner for this particular product category. Years later however, the vision was beautifully realized and distributed worldwide.

Ariadne's Dream wallpaper & fabric design by Kim Parker

No Elephants in the Garden

On a hot summer's evening under a full moon in Union Square, I came across a woman selling lovely hand painted amulets with fairies on them. I decided to purchase one. I wore it around my neck for a few weeks. I felt that it had a special energy and power. The magical depiction of a fairy inspired me to create my first children's book that I titled "The Flower Fairy."

Whenever a creative idea would come into my head, I would go into an exhaustive tailspin until the vision was completed. For a few weeks I was deeply immersed in the project. The story became an autobiographical tale about a fairy whose mission was to heal the world by canvassing everything with her flowers. When the manuscript was finished Felipe contacted an editor at Scholastic to set up a book meeting.

Andrea, a young editor at Scholastic met with us in her office full of delightful children's book titles and shelves full of stuffed animals. After looking through my manuscript, she said:

"Your illustrations are lovely, Kim. Unfortunately we just completed a book about fairies. Would you consider re-illustrating another book already in the public domain?"

My immediate reaction to this question was that every book that I had ever really loved as a child was cherished mostly because I had grown very fond of its illustrations. Maurice Sendak, Dr. Seuss, and Louisa May Alcott were just a few examples of great illustrators whose artwork left a lovely impression upon me. I adored the British classic: "The Secret Garden" with its very beautiful drawings of young companions Mary and Dickon amid lush English garden settings. I couldn't imagine replacing such classic illustrations with my own.

"What about an ABC Book or a Counting Book?" Andrea asked. "Would you be willing to illustrate one of those kinds of children's books instead?"

I knew I had so many magical stories I wanted to share with children. A counting book or an ABC book seemed to me like such a dull idea. But without really feeling inspired by her suggestion, I automatically replied, "I can give it a try."

When I got home that night I spoke to my mother about it.

"Kim, I think you will enjoy illustrating a counting book, especially because you won't have to deal with the text and the frustration of editor's changing your words all of the time. A counting book would just be about your beautiful illustrations and you'll have more freedom," she said. "Take a look at Eric Carle's books. See how successful he has become as a children's book illustrator with all of his charming collages."

I took my mother's suggestion and went directly to the Barnes & Noble on Union Square to browse the books of Eric Carle. I didn't have children so I was not familiar with his work. My mother's suggestion to look at his ABC and counting books helped inspire my new book project because they were colorful and unique.

Andrea suggested I show her just a few sample pages of my new counting book to start.

"Just give me numbers 1-3," she instructed.

I knew the importance of showing a complete and finished artistic vision to anyone. Bringing something half-baked could sell a vision short, leading to possible rejection in my experience. So I dove directly into the pool. I spent the next few weeks at my dining room table illustrating the entire book without knowing whether it would be published. I painted numbers 1-10, front and back covers and even the end pages. A few days later I took it to a meeting with Andrea.

The concept behind, "Counting in the Garden," was inspired by our wild tabby cat Rudy who had a nasty habit of hiding underneath our Victorian sofa and then darting out suddenly, biting our ankles with his sharp teeth. He was always up to no good. We had adopted him as a lost kitten off of the New York City streets one cold winter. And although we grew to adore his unpredictable, wild nature, there was a bit of an unpleasant price attached. But had it not been for his mischievous personality, I might not have come up with the concept for my first children's book. I painted animals cleverly hidden amid lush garden settings. It would be visually challenging for kids to find them amid the flowers.

A few days later Andrea called me. "We would like to take your "Counting in the Garden" manuscript to a Florida book fair if that's OK? If we receive interest in it, we will offer you a book deal," she said. That seemed fair to me.

When the Florida book fair was over, Andrea let us know that "Counting in the Garden" received an order for 10,000 units in its dummy manuscript form.

"We will send you your contract and book advance shortly," she told me.

At the same time that I'd just received the good news, she added,

"I have a request from my boss Kevin. He wants you to remove the elephant illustrations from the book and replace them with another animal. He feels that elephants don't belong in a garden. He also wants you to take out the sheep and snakes. He feels that parents simply won't be able to explain to their children why there is an elephant or a sheep standing in a garden. He also thinks that your snakes are too phallic- looking."

I wondered whether I was hearing this correctly? The head of a children's book imprint could not allow an elephant to stand in a garden? What about Dumbo who flew with his ears? What about Babar who wore a business suit and tie? Wasn't a child's world a magical, imaginative landscape where anything could take place?

I felt upset. The elephants were my favorite part of the book, illustrated with so much love.

"Andrea," I said, "The elephants are really the heart of my book. I love them. I painted them the way children in India see them everyday. Each one is decorated with colors and patterns on their backs. They are lovingly holding each other's tails with their trunks full of flowers. What would be so hard for a child or parent to understand about that?"

There was a short and awkward period of silence. "I am sorry Kim, but you will have to remove them, as well as the sheep and snakes. If you cannot do this, there will be no book, " she said.

After we got off the phone I called my father whose anger I suddenly found quite refreshing. Throughout my childhood, my father had read me many children's books when he came home from work. Our favorite story was

Dr. Seuss's "Thidwick the Big Hearted Moose," a book whose moral was: "Don't let others take advantage of you."

"What a total f'nmoron!" he shouted. "He missed the whole God damn point! Those elephants were beautiful. They were the heart of your book! He is basically ripping it right the hell out! "

My father reacted at that moment in a way I could not have done with Andrea. I was actually comforted by his outrage. Right after that, I phoned my Buddhist healer, Gil. Gil and I had been working together for almost twenty years. I knew he would offer me sound advice about how to process and handle the situation.

"Gil," I said while crying, "How can I remove the elephants from the garden when they were painted with so much love? I feel like my heart is being ripped out."

Gil said gently, "I know, it makes no sense that such a man could be seated at the head of a children's book imprint and not see the beauty and the love in those magical illustrations of yours. But going forward darling, when you sit down to paint those new creatures, don't think about him. Just think of the *children* who will ultimately be holding your beautiful book one day. Just think of the gift you will be giving to them. They will feel your love."

Soon afterward, I sat down at the dining room table with Gil's wise words and soft voice in my heart. I painted new animals to replace the elephants, sheep and snakes. He was right. The book *was* for the children. It was not for Kevin. I replaced elephants with playful dogs, sheep with bunny rabbits, and snakes with vividly winged butterflies.

And a year later, when the box of newly bound *Counting in the Garden* books were delivered to our front door, I must admit, it was as if Heaven had arrived. Upon opening that box, the sight of those crisp white books was a moment of personal triumph and joy. They were sparkling like jewels before my eyes with a big pink flower on the cover. I thought of Gil's magical words. I held them in my hands and hugged and kissed them like precious children.

Counting in the Garden was published in 2005 and received rave reviews and endorsements from PBS.org, Publishers Weekly, School Library Journal, The New York Times and Kirkus Reviews. They called it a "sleeper hit" at the Frankfurt Book Fair. It spawned a children's brand, Kim Parker Kids ® that Scholastic Media licensed for the following five years, a line of adorable plush toys, stationery, backpacks and puppets and was then translated into Spanish and Arabic.

Cover of *Counting in the Garden*

(Scholastic 2005)

Mums and Asters

Our very first designer rug licensing partnership for the Kim Parker brand, was with a company that produced beautiful hand woven Nepalese rugs. I was definitely excited to see my floral designs transformed into lush, high- end wool carpets. We quickly signed a contract in those early licensing days, that ultimately turned out to be very poorly written and a bad move. Let us call it a painful early lesson in the business that taught us about protective, contractual language and the importance of having an "exit clause." Without one, you might be tied in forever with a company that is dishonest or unethical.

That first rug company actually produced very beautiful quality Tibetan wool rugs that featured my floral designs. The rugs got great press coverage in Elle Décor magazine, Oprah's "O Magazine" and Interior Design magazine. However, because that first contract was so poorly written, we encountered many problems, and kicking free was one of the most painful business experiences to date.

A few months after we terminated with our first rug manufacturer, on an extremely freezing cold, January evening while driving through the dark, sub- zero Soho streets in my brother's Jeep, my sister in law asked whether I would like to jump out of the car and join her for a fast stroll down Wooster Street. In truth, I was not thrilled with this invitation to go out into the bitter cold weather. But I went to keep her company. Suddenly a brightly lit storefront window appeared before my eyes. It was decorated with beautiful hand woven rugs on full display. I instantly recognized one of them because it was the black and white floral rug that had been featured in ELLE Décor magazine right beside my own, months earlier. I told my sister in law I wanted to just pop into the rug store before it closed and that I'd be right back.

Greeted kindly by a young and friendly British salesperson at the entrance, I immediately noticed a copy of the actual issue of Elle Décor magazine right there on the coffee table in their showroom. I opened it to the exact page where my "Zinnias" designer rug had been featured alongside one of their designer rugs.

"Can I help you?" The salesperson asked politely.

I held the issue of Elle Décor up and said, "This is my designer rug, and I am actually looking for a new rug manufacturer." He explained that the owners of the company were based in London. "I would be happy to pass on your business card and contact information to them right away," he said cheerfully.

"Thank you, that would be lovely!" I said. I thanked him, shook his hand and we said goodnight.

What I later learned from The Rug Company president himself, was that he had actually seen my "Zinnias" rug featured in that Elle Décor issue and apparently had gone to some lengths to contact my former rug licensing partner in hopes of possibly collaborating with me. However, not surprisingly, he was not given any contact information from them.

"I am coming to New York in a week," he told me from London. "Let's arrange to meet at that time." A week later we met in his Soho showroom.

The Rug Company president was an elegant, soft spoken, British man, not much older than me. I brought along a few of my hardcover books that were full of professional, glossy photos documenting my hand painted textile designs. I thought initially that this might be an easier way for him to view my large body of work. I also brought along a suitcase filled with my hand painted silk designs.

"What's in your case?" he asked.

"My original textile designs," I said.

"Great. Let's have a look at them," he said smiling.

We sat together on the sofa where I opened up my portfolio case, full of my original hand painted silk textile designs. Holding a few of them gently he said:

"These are all brilliant." We then sat quietly selecting initial floral and geometric designs together that we felt would look best on designer rugs. A few days later he sent me a contract. This began a highly successful and bestselling decade-long designer collaboration with The Rug Company of London.

The Rug Company had worldwide distribution through various showrooms from the US, Europe, Mexico, to Dubai. They produced the absolute finest quality rugs in the design industry. They had a healthy advertising budget to promote their designer rugs in countless fashion and design publications globally every month. My rugs were featured in major fashion and design publications around the world from Vogue, The World of Interiors, Architectural Digest France and Germany, Living Etc., ELLE Décor, Elle Decoration UK to Veranda and many more.

Their Soho showroom resembled a gallery with fine rug tapestries hanging like works of art from high ceilings against white walls. They also represented iconic fashion designers such as: Sir Paul Smith, Vivienne Westwood, Diane Von Furstenberg, Marni, to name a few.

Their rugs were beautifully hand crafted, all woven with the finest Tibetan wool. Each would require four months to create. My hand painted textile designs were executed with absolute integrity upon these rugs; every spontaneous hand painted detail magnificently captured by their extraordinary artisans in India.

Although I had a huge archive of designs, we initially agreed to focus solely on advertising and promoting just two floral rugs to start. I named one of them "Mums and Asters," and the other "Tea Roses." They were both professionally photographed and showcased in elegant room interiors that appeared in ads that were run many times in design and fashion publications worldwide. "Mums and Asters" became an iconic rug design in the industry.

Sales started rolling in. In a year's time, "Mums and Asters" became an industry bestseller. It won three prestigious international British design awards for "Best in Flooring Design," and was very tastefully editorialized in countless fashion and lifestyle design publications. "Mums and Asters" was also featured prominently on Carrie Bradshaw's bedroom floor in the first "Sex and the City" movie. It was so popular that it was even at the center of three copyright infringement lawsuits with major rug company competitors who wished to capitalize on its success.

Over the course of our ten-year designer collaboration, we developed more than ten rugs together both floral and geometric for the collection. They all received substantial press coverage and sales were strong.

One afternoon I received a call from one of the salespeople at their Soho store that Academy-award winning Director, Peter Jackson of Lord of the Rings, had stopped into The Rug Company's New York showroom with his wife and purchased all of my designer rugs for their New Zealand home. They had even placed a special order requesting that one of my fine art floral panel paintings (that had been a popular image in the category of wall art reproduction for ten years) also be turned into a rug for their home as well.

And after ten years of a highly successful designer collaboration, with bestselling rugs worldwide, we parted ways. New contractual terms unfortunately led to an impasse, and ten years of success, were swept under the carpet.

Mums and Asters by Kim Parker

41 Madison Avenue and Spode

Forty-One Madison Avenue is the tabletop industry flagship building in New York City. I renamed that tall modern black glass building "Mount Everest." Slender like a cigarette lighter and looming over the southeast corner of 26th Street and Madison Square Park, it houses all of the top dinnerware companies around the world from Lifetime Brands, Rosenthal, Wedgewood, Spode, Lenox and Richard Ginori. For years, Felipe and I had visited various showrooms in search of the perfect tabletop licensing partner, and met with countless company Presidents and Design Directors.

The very first tabletop collections I designed in 2001 were for Block China. I met them at the licensing show at the Javitz Center. They were one of our very first licensing partners. I designed eight tabletop collections for that first dinnerware launch.

Designing my first dinnerware collections for Block China was a new and very pleasant experience. I was given free reign to create what I felt would look pretty on a dinner plate template, bowl, mug or pitcher. When looking back, there was a lot to learn. One early lesson was that when a Chinese factory is repainting one of your original hand painted designs, a lot of your own original style gets lost in translation in that process. The designs no longer look as if painted by your hand.

The Block China showroom on 41 Madison Avenue was brightly lit on the eve of our dinnerware launch. The pieces were displayed in elegant glass cases for the retail buyers during market week. The very first launch of my dinnerware collections however, fell on 9-11. The city was empty. The world was in a state of total shock and of course, no buyers were flying into New York City to see these collections.

Three years later, when the contract with Block China had ended, with few commitments at retail, we looked to partner with another dinnerware company. After visiting several showrooms and meeting several tabletop executives at 41 Madison Avenue, Spode, a classic English company, became our next dinnerware, licensing partner. By this time, we had a great deal of UK press, with three British design awards to our credit, largely due to our bestselling collaboration with The Rug Company of London.

Spode was a wonderful partner for our brand. I had absolute creative freedom with them as well to create two large dinnerware collections just as I had envisioned them. Their Design Director was extremely enthusiastic about these new patterns. Spode had a Royal Warrant to produce dinnerware for the Royal Family. It was an English dinnerware company steeped in tradition, for a few hundred years. The new patterns I had created were anything but traditionally English. They were bold and exuberant, not typically dainty like most English dinnerware. My collections would be a new look and departure from the patterns they had been selling.

Opening night at 41 Madison Avenue in the Spode showroom was memorable. My collections were introduced beside Jamie Oliver's new line of cookware. Buyers from retail, editors of many of the top industry publications were at the opening and viewing my new collections in the showroom.

One of the sweetest moments, as we entered the lobby of 41 Madison Avenue that evening, was seeing that the cover of the industry's most popular dinnerware publication, HFN featured my "Emma's Garland" rosy, floral dinner plate right on the front cover the caption beside it read: "A New York Plate of Mind."

Opening night was a champagne and hors d'oeuvres evening and special event with hundreds of buyers and editors. Macy's committed instantly to carrying both of my floral dinnerware collections. Other retailers such as Belk, Dillard's, JC Penney and Harrods signed on too. At the end of opening night, Felipe and I and the entire Spode team celebrated privately in the showroom eating roast beef sandwiches, shrimp and delicious home baked goods, hugging, laughing and taking delight in the success of the launch.

Our Spode collaboration lasted three years, however, in our third year, during a bad recession, sadly, Spode encountered (as many companies were at that time) financial unforeseen challenges that led to the temporary closing of the company.

James McEnearny

One of the things I cherished most while growing up in our Long Island, New York home was that our living room had a library full of beautiful art books. From an early age my mother and I would curl up on the couch looking at books on Vuillard, Bonnard and Matisse. I believe that the paintings of Vuillard deeply inspired and influenced my own future design aesthetic of layering richly colored patterns inside the home.

With collections of wallpaper, fabrics, bedding, bath, designer rugs, pillows, tableware, wall art and giftware being distributed worldwide, I felt inspired to create an art and design book. This was no easy undertaking. I felt slightly overwhelmed at first. I knew I didn't want to create the typical "How To Decorate" book, and I was not interested in telling people how to hang a curtain. There were many colorful industry stories that I wanted to tell.

Our dear ninety-year old neighborhood friend Jim, an Irish playwright from the South Bronx became my unofficial editor as did Felipe. We met Jim in front of his stoop on East 17th Street and Irving Place. For years, Jim sold his collection of first edition books to passersby at the foot of his landmark brownstone's stoop. The money he had made from book sales he generously donated to the local hospice where his beloved late wife Pauline had passed away.

Jim was a handsome, Irish man with a truly infectious love for life. He was *the* quintessential New Yorker, riding the bus to Lincoln Center where he would sit by the fountain in front of the Henry Moore sculpture, reading a book by himself on a hot summer's day. He frequented independent film houses all over the city calling us afterward and recommending documentary films he had just seen. The three of us walked the city streets together, Jim on one of my arms and Felipe on the other. He would often say in his protective deep voice, "Felipe, Kim is the rose and we are the thorns." When we adopted Wendy, our second beloved dog as a puppy, we took her directly to his brownstone for approval. "You three are a family now," he said endearingly, without hesitation.

On hot summer evenings, we sat together on his front stoop people-watching, and greeting familiar neighborhood faces. He was a great observer of the city's local color sharing a mutual love for New York City life. Stopping me before a tree in Gramercy Park in spring he pointed to flowers, asking innocently, "Kim, can you please tell me what these are called?" His childlike curiosity at ninety was one of his most lovable traits.

Throughout the time I was writing the text, both Jim and Felipe gave me tremendous positive feedback, valid criticism and support. Jim's brownstone was just a five- minute walk from ours. Once a chapter was finished, I would walk it over and slide an envelope thru the mail slot of his old front door. Hours later he would call me by phone with his feedback. "Kim, this is pure Dickens," he once told me. "It is evident that everything you ever achieved in your life was hard earned, never handed to you."

He was a wonderful storyteller, sitting every morning at our local neighborhood café writing in his own journal with shaking hands, in his illegible scrawl. He would invite us to join him there for what he would call "a dolce," ("*something sweet*") generously treating us to lunches when the moment moved him. On my birthday we dined together at the French Culinary Institute in Soho.

The poor boy from the South Bronx had cleverly invested his money over the course of his life, in beer and coffee stocks. It was an investment that eventually paid handsome dividends that he enjoyed sharing with us.

Growing a Spine

With several home furnishing collections on the market, from designer rugs, dinnerware, bedding, bath, wall art and stationery, and with thousands of original hand painted textile designs and painted garden and abstract canvases, I threw myself into designing my first art book. As usual, once an idea entered my head, I would be consumed until completion.

This was no small project. I spent two years amassing photographs and putting this book together thoughtfully. The text would be memoir. Once my three ring binder manuscript had been finished, Felipe contacted top New York publishing houses that produced beautiful coffee table books.

Each publisher had a particular formula. In truth, none of the other design books I had seen on the shelves at Barnes and Noble looked like mine. My binder was filled with floral paintings, textile designs and home furnishings, as well as photographs of urban gardens and flea market color that I had taken in the New York City streets on my camera.

After just a few initial meetings with editors, most of whom didn't understand my vision for the book, I was starting to lose confidence. Some publishers wanted me to copy the formats and formulas that other of my design colleagues had already produced. None liked the idea of the text being memoir. One editor even sarcastically said:

"And where shall we carry your book? In the design section or the memoir section?"

I just wanted to tell my colorful New York City stories - accompanied by my colorful collections.

One Sunday evening, Felipe and I received an email from one of the top industry book publishers. I knew very little about her. What I had heard however was that she had the "Midas touch" when it came to selling books. Other publishers told me that all of her books became bestsellers. I was also informed that she was a "tough cookie." The books she published ranged from celebrated celebrities and designers to porn stars. She had her own imprint and was an industry powerhouse. Her email was relatively short and direct, received on a Sunday evening. She had heard about my manuscript and asked whether she could have a look at it. The email had no salutation. This struck us both as somewhat uncivilized.

Two days later, we found ourselves headed uptown in a cab to her office off of Fifth Avenue. Not surprisingly, her office was impressive with grand views. Greeted by her two young female assistants, we were asked to sit at her conference room table, and place the heavy three-ring binder there. One of the assistants took an initial look through it.

"Your work is really beautiful. I know that she is going to love this," she said.

The Queen of Bestsellers entered the room, in faded blue jeans, blue jean sleeveless vest and belly button hanging out. Impatiently she said:

"All right, let's see the manuscript." It was there upon the table.

Flipping quickly through it in less than two minutes, she said:

"OK, this is what we would do if we were to work together." Asking one of her assistants to pull an existing design book off her shelf, a large - sized coffee table book on fashion designer Vivian Tam. She continued:

"This is an example of what we could do for you. I'd have to get someone to rewrite your entire text. I would hire a professional photographer to reshoot the interiors with your designer collections. None of the photographs in this binder are good enough. All you designers think you're photographers. We'd have to start from scratch," she said.

I took a deep breath. As much as I appreciated her professional opinion, and her interest in creating a polished looking coffee table book on design, I knew right away that we were not on the same page. I had a vision. It took me two years to create it. I was not looking for some shiny coffee table book, like so many I'd seen on the design shelves at book stores.

I never claimed to be a photographer. However, many of the photos in the dummy book of our home interior were actually shot professionally by a photographer for the London Guardian. I just wanted the book to reflect my Bohemian life in New York City, and to share my story.

I knew at that moment that this publisher was not the one. Getting to my feet on the other side of the conference room table, I reached across to shake her hand.

"Thank you, and I appreciate your time, " I said, "but I honestly don't think we should work on this book project together."

"I couldn't work with you, either," she replied gruffly.

Felipe and I were always avid city walkers. That day after the meeting, we walked home down Fifth Avenue and it felt like we were flying. In other words, I couldn't walk fast enough out of there. Many other publishing meetings followed. I knew that it would take a very special set of eyes to see my vision. I waited patiently for the right publisher.

Harry N. Abrams

When my publishing odyssey began, the very first art book publisher we approached was Harry N. Abrams. In my childhood living room, the bookshelves were full of many beautiful Abrams art books. I remember seeing the word Abrams on their spines. We had books on Cezanne, Renoir, Manet and countless other great painters that were all published by Harry N. Abrams. They were clearly one of the finest art book publishing houses in the world.

When bringing my manuscript to my first meeting with Abrams on West 18th Street, I met with a young editor there who also loved painting flowers. She enthusiastically spent thoughtful time reviewing my manuscript and seemed to emotionally understand what I was trying to manifest. She held onto the manuscript for three entire months. When we met again she said kindly, "I understand what you are trying to create here, Kim. I just think you need to give it a bit more time and a bit more work." Explaining ways in which it could potentially be reformatted, she said, "Come back in six months, and we will look at it again. I think you're well on your way."

During that year, I worked extremely hard every day reformatting pages and editing stories. My friend Michaela, a talented designer, who had graduated from Cooper Union, suggested helpful ways in which to organize the manuscript's presentation.

And after a year of reworking it, I returned to Abrams. This time we met with a seasoned editor who had been with the publisher for twenty something years. She was a very kind woman who sat quietly with the manuscript in front of her, taking careful and thoughtful time looking through it. After fifteen quiet minutes, placing her hands over the cover, she said warmly:

"Now *this* is a book! It's wonderful that your text is your story, Kim. You have had such courage. I feel your story will inspire other women around the world to follow their dreams. I love your dinnerware collections for Spode, and your rugs are stunning."

I could hardly believe my ears. I told her how many publishers we had met with over the course of the past year and a half. I mentioned our meeting on Fifth Avenue with the Queen of Bestsellers.

"Kim, I have to tell you," she said shaking her head smiling, "You are truly one in a million. Most designers would have done the book with her just to get published. She turns everything into bestsellers, you know. She might have offered you a huge advance too. Abrams could never match such an advance—but, you Kim, will *always* be an *Abrams author*," she said with a knowing smile.

Suddenly the image of all of the Abrams art books that had graced our living room shelves throughout my childhood, appeared in my mind. No advance could mean more to me than that.

A week or so later, the contract and advance were sent to me. A very difficult process was about to begin. Three months into the contract this lovely, seasoned editor who had signed me on sent me an email saying that she had been offered another job at another publishing house. She would now be handing the manuscript over to someone else.

I was naturally disappointed. She seemed to me like such a rare bird in the publishing industry. I'd not met anyone like her. She truly understood the manuscript's vision, and openly encouraged me to tell my stories.

After her departure I was called in to meet with the publisher of Abrams. I had not yet met her. She had just come off of a plane trip that cold, rainy morning from London. Visibly sick, coughing, and definitely not in the best of health. She asked us to sit down in her office. Without hesitation she said:

"We cannot publish your book," A dead silence followed. I was not sure how to respond. An advance and contract had already been issued, and for the past three months, I had been reworking the manuscript as per the suggestions of the original editor.

"I have never seen a design book that is *also* a memoir," she said sternly. "You have a fan base as a designer. They want you to tell them how to decorate. It's your responsibility as the designer to provide your followers with tips and helpful decorating hints. The text cannot be a memoir. We wouldn't even know how to market such a book! Should we sell it in the "gardening section" where there are flowers? Should we sell it in the "design section" or the "memoir section?" she asked sarcastically.

She did not understand my vision. Felipe instantly suggested a change in the title that would more commercially help sell the book. But even though she liked his suggestion, it was pretty clear, she didn't understand the entire vision, and was ready to kill it.

When I got home from the meeting, I found myself reaching out to my Buddhist healer Gil, once again, for his wisdom and sound advice. Gil knew well how important this book had been to me. He knew how much time and love had been invested in it. I had already received my advance and contract.

As always, Gil provided me with the perfect advice:

"Release it honey," he said to me gently. "Email this publisher. Tell her in just a few simple words that the language in your contract clearly states that this publishing project is "a *collaboration*." If she does not understand the meaning of the word "collaboration" then you must ask her to "please release me from this contract."

At first it felt like I could never do that. It took me a while to process Gil's words. I wondered how I could be released from such an important and meaningful project with so much time invested in it?

Taking a deep breath though, I did as Gil had advised. I composed a short email stating just what Gil had said. I hit the "send" button, grabbed Felipe and said: "Let's walk the East River." That was where we always went when we wanted a feeling of openness and to clear our heads. Interestingly, I felt an instant sense of freedom not long after hitting the send button. Fear was replaced immediately with deep relief. Gil was right. Letting go was liberating. A few days later, the publisher emailed saying, "We will publish your book. We will do it your way."

However, it was a long and difficult year, after that. I fought hard for every single word, story, and photo to remain true to my vision. Like my old Irish friend Jim had said, "Everything you ever achieved was hard won, Kim."

Agreeing to "collaborate" meant that I would include design inspirations and helpful tips in the text, but we agreed that the front of the book could be part memoir.

Kim Parker Home: A Life in Design was published in the Spring of 2008 and the book received the largest book club order in the history of the imprint with an order of about 13,000 units that instantly sent the book into a second printing. The London Times gave it a rave review, as did the UK Press Association, Living Etc. and it was endorsed by Vanity Fair.

Our book launch party was a magical evening held at the beautiful National Arts Club on Gramercy Park in its elegant Victorian interior amid friends and design industry colleagues.

The book's publication led to brilliant friendships and inspiring letters from as far away as Thailand, Australia, France and Korea, to Slovenia and Brazil. And just as the first, seasoned editor had predicted, emails from women around the world thanking me for having the courage to follow my dreams, inspired them to follow their own creative paths, and the book continues to be the gift that keeps on giving.

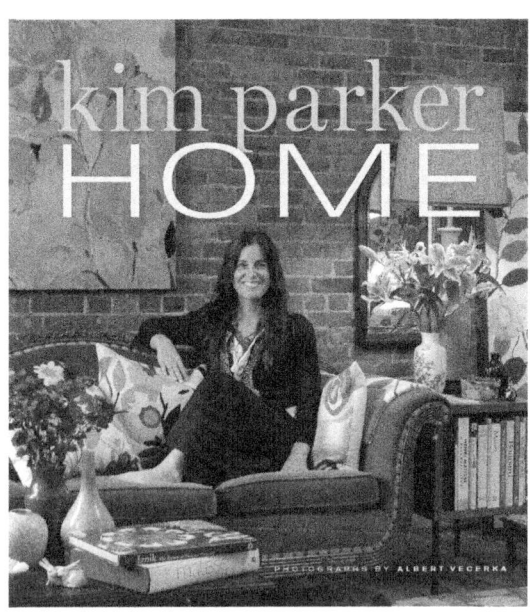

A Visit From Jim Thompson

Jim Thompson is one of the largest silk fabric companies in the world, and is located in Thailand. A few years after my design book was published, I received an email from its Design Director Harold in Thailand that read:

"In all of the years that I have been Design Director here at Jim Thompson, I have never come across such beautiful work in all my life. Kim, you are our modern day Matisse."

He told me he had my design book with him in Bangkok and that he was planning a short trip to New York and wanted to schedule a meeting. He was interested, he said, in a co-branded designer collaboration with the Jim Thompson brand. We discussed producing silk fabrics, and fashion accessories to be distributed all over Asia, the US and Europe in the Jim Thompson showrooms featuring my floral designs.

One afternoon in Union Square, ten years before Harold paid me a visit (right after I had stopped selling my designs to the fashion industry namelessly), Felipe spotted a woman in a silk blouse walking with a friend through the farmer's market. Her silk blouse had one of my hand painted floral designs printed on it. I recognized this design instantly too, but could not remember to whom I had sold that particular silk floral print on her blouse all those years ago.

The next thing I knew Felipe was greeting her and enquiring where she had bought it.

"It was a present from my partner to me when she was in Thailand shopping at Jim Thompson. You know Jim Thompson, don't you?" she asked. Neither of us knew who Jim Thompson was at that time.

"He has the most beautiful silk empire of fabrics and silk products in stores all over Asia," she said. "He is very famous. My partner bought me this blouse as a gift when she was vacationing in Thailand."

"The floral print on your blouse was painted by my wife," Felipe said.

The woman looked at me with a smile. The next thing I knew, she was actually offering me the blouse off her back.

"That's extremely kind of you," I said with a slight feeling of embarrassment. "But we were just curious as to where your blouse had been made. There is no need to give it to me, but thank you so much for this truly kind gesture."

After many attempts she said:

"I really feel there is a reason that you should have this blouse. Meet me at my hotel in an hour if you can, and I will give it to you."

Two hours later we met at her hotel. I brought her an embroidered floral pillow from my collection as a gift in exchange. Even though her blouse was not my size, I accepted it, wondering why it wound up in my possession.

Almost eight entire years after this encounter, the Design Director at Jim Thompson from Thailand walked through my Gramercy Park apartment door into our brownstone living room. Harold was a tall and distinguished man in his mid sixties. I instantly guessed his astrological sign of Pisces.

"How did you know that?" he asked.

"There is something ethereal about you," I explained, "You have a mystical Piscean aura."

We spent the next four hours looking through literally hundreds of my hand painted silk textile designs, and even fine art canvases, discussing our vision for a Kim Parker for Jim Thompson silk fabric line. I was exhausted after this four hour meeting, but in the best sense. We sat at my dining room table sipping tea and eating cookies when I suddenly had the feeling that this was all an apparition; that none of this was actually happening. Harold's mystical aura was unlike anyone else's I had ever met. When he walked through the front door I felt as if I had been meeting with a ghost, a spirit, not an actual man for some reason. I saw a kind of white "light" surrounding him as he entered. He had such a soft nature. He was generous and warm, and there was a definite feeling of harmony and calm instantly between us.

Jim Thompson was the company founder, who established this amazing silk empire in Bangkok in the 1950's to worldwide success. Mysteriously, a few decades later, Jim Thompson was out walking one day in the jungle thicket, and never returned. He disappeared into thin air, no one ever seeing him again. There were allegations that he was a CIA spy, but the mystery of his disappearance was never solved.

"I really want this collaboration to happen," Harold said. "I need to warn you though. Please be very careful during the contract negotiations. The VP of the company is all about numbers. You will make a fortune with us. I guarantee it. You will be able to produce everything you ever dreamed of on silk and have it made into garments and products of your choice. It will be sold worldwide through our many outlets."

He took my hand across the table tenderly, looking me deeply in the eyes.

"Kim," he said, "I have never seen so much beauty and talent in all of my years as a Design Director. It was an honor to meet you."

After four hours, we were saying goodbye and hugging at the front door. "Our attorney will contact you," he said, and then he left.

As soon as the door closed, I turned to Felipe and said, "Did that just happen?" Felipe looked at me and said, "I understand what you mean. There was something really unusual about this meeting."

Weeks later we received a contract that was not too detailed in language nor as thorough and protective as most of our licensing contracts had been. I knew I could never sign such a document. It needed the usual tweaking and protective language we had become accustomed to. But after just a few email exchanges between lawyers, suddenly there was a deafening silence. Their attorney stopped writing. Harold did too. And just like that, it was over.

Like the disappearance of Jim Thompson himself, Harold was also now missing in action. I had to process this mysterious ending without disappointment, which wasn't easy as the idea of creating all of those beautiful products on silk was a dream. I was not sure whether our attorney's suggestions to tweak the language in the existing contract scared their lawyer away, or whether the whole encounter was just some kind of mirage. I wondered whether Harold was in fact the reincarnation of Jim Thompson himself, respectfully visiting me that day.

I would never forget Harold's gentle and elegant presence. His generous words about my work really seemed to genuinely come from spirit. In his first email to me he had written: "I can see going through your book, that we belong together," and finally, "We have exactly what each other needs and the possibilities are endless."

A Bloomingdale's Launch

One snowy New York City evening we were invited to Bloomingdale's to attend a very special party for "The New American Spirit" campaign, which was a part of the launch of my new bedding and bath collections at this renowned retailer.

We were picked up in a limo in blizzard-like conditions and taken uptown to 59th Street and Lexington Avenue, arranged by our bedding company's VP, Jean, to ensure timely arrival. I was to be introduced to the President of Bloomingdale's.

All I remember about that sparkling evening was how the Bloomingdale's President told me that our bedding collections had "made history"- selling out in record time. He openly expressed his delight in seeing my floral patterns on the bedding floor, only a few feet away from Calvin Klein's very sleek and solid black, masculine style aesthetic, and bedding collections by Ralph Lauren and Donna Karan. Escorting me to another section of the store, he proudly showed me a new furniture line they were launching that evening as well.

The launch was going along nicely, until suddenly, with a glass of wine still in one hand, I was swiftly being whisked away like Cinderella from the ball, and from conversation with the Bloomingdale's President, down the escalator to the main floor. Jean had taken my arm firmly, saying, "We have to leave now." (as if I would soon turn into the girl in rags and my coach into a pumpkin.) I wasn't sure why I was being rushed away not long after arrival. The evening was turning out well. The blizzard however, could not have been worse that night.

To my surprise, Jean led me to the Vera Wang perfume counter on the main floor where she generously purchased a bottle of her latest fragrance for me as a kind of celebratory gift for the success of the launch. I was touched by this unexpected gesture.

However, we didn't go home together in the limo that evening. Instead, Felipe and I were left at the Bloomingdale's entrance unable to get a taxi in the snowstorm. Taxis were nowhere to be found on such a miserable night. So in our formal attire and dress shoes, hand in hand, we walked through the mounting high drifts of snow, in blizzard-like conditions all the way down Lexington Avenue and 59th Street to our apartment on East 18th Street in Gramercy Park. We held each other's frost bitten hands every step of the icy way, laughing and reminiscing about the evening's joyful events while snow mounted on our coats and shoes, carefully making our way home through grey, slushy, icy mounds.

During that three-year designer collaboration, I learned a lot about the categories of bedding and bath. Licensing was still very new to us at that early stage of our brand. As with all of our first licensing partnerships, we learned where our strengths and our weaknesses were, and where we belonged in the market. Certain floral designs translated better on a shower curtain than on a comforter. Fabrications needed to be selected carefully as their qualities could negatively or positively affect the integrity of the product. The wrong colored accent pillow on a bed could visually ruin the beauty of an entire ensemble. A particular design that had become a bestseller on a rug, didn't necessarily work as successfully upon a bed or a shower curtain. Honing in on the right scale of a hand painted design, color combination, and fabrication were decisions that ultimately led to the success or failure of any bedding collection.

Our first bedding collections at Bloomingdale's sold out in record time. We ultimately learned that operating solely in the high end of the retail market meant having a limited financial reach to the consumer. But the pleasure of seeing one's vision realized on high-end bedding at Bloomingdale's, during that very first year that our brand was introduced, would always remain an early, and sweet triumph.

Trade Shows and Horses

When the economic recession hit the US in 2008, many companies in the design industry had limited budgets and could not afford to sign on for designer collaborations. It didn't matter whether you had already partnered with the finest companies, won three design awards, had industry bestselling collections, or goods sold in every major retailer. Most companies were basically only able to put their money down on celebrity branded products, going behind anyone that was on television.

I remembered one of my favorite writers, Frank McCourt once saying in a sarcastic manner when interviewed after winning the Pulitzer Prize for *Angela's Ashes*, "You're basically a nobody unless you are on TV."

Those of us who had been designing all of our lives were suddenly being replaced on retail shelves by TV personalities like singer Donny Osmond who suddenly became bedding and bath designers.

During this time, we were researching our options for the next partnership. We displayed our goods at trade shows, placed ads in magazines. New York City clearly looked like it was in a state of slow decay. Once pretty little shops were now boarded- up, and small businesses had lost their leases.

The truth is, I couldn't stand trade shows. Designer colleagues had investors providing them capital for the largest amount of floor space at a show, situating their booths front and center to ensure maximum traffic.

The very first trade show we participated in was the Licensing Show in 2001 at the Jacob Javitz Center for the launch of my namesake brand. It actually went well for us. Numerous companies signed us on. A few years later, Scholastic Media, who represented Kim Parker Kids, promoted our children's brand right alongside their biggest licensed property, Clifford the Red Dog.

During the recession, however, with not a whole lot going on, we semi-reluctantly decided to commit ourselves to another trade show at the Javitz Center to try and drum up new business. The Boutique Design Show targeted buyers from hotels around the world looking for unique home furnishings such as pillows, rugs and wall art for their hospitality properties. If just one small or large hotel decided to order a few thousand pillows, or rugs, it could be a lucrative deal.

What I remember best, however, about that trade show, had nothing to do with the trade show. After setting up our booth at the Javitz Center a day before it kicked off, while walking from 11th to 10th Avenue, heading back downtown towards home, we came upon an old, dark garage that was actually a very old carriage house. Beautiful horses were kept there after their long, brutal hours pulling tourists around Central Park by carriage.

One such sweet horse was tied very closely to a wall on the outside of this carriage house. It barely had enough length on his chain to bob his poor unhappy head. Tears instantly flooded my eyes. It was unbearable to me. I could not stand seeing such a beautiful animal cruelly chained so tightly to a wall. I gently patted his soft nose and kissed it. I dared to venture inside his dark and dingy stable, where I quickly grabbed a small handful of pellets from a large feeding bin inside for him.

A white-haired man with Irish accent, clad in knickers and an old-fashioned carriage driver's outfit, suddenly appeared like someone out of a Thomas Hardy novel. "Off with ye!" he shouted. He clearly didn't want me to see the filthy conditions of his horse's stable nor show any degree of affection for this poor, overworked creature.

I cried all the way home in the cab that day. I felt sickened and infuriated. It was that encounter that led me to get involved in petitions against those horse-drawn carriages along Central Park South that I had always hated near The Plaza Hotel. These beautiful animals were literally enslaved, standing in brutal summer heat and frigid winter cold. They were forced to pull tourists through New York City traffic, breathing in bus fumes and dodging taxis, with no quality of life, no reward, nor freedom in their lives to be the Divine creatures they were meant to be. They would spend hours and hours on their feet with no relief, all clearly verging on physical and emotional exhaustion and often collapse and death.

As it turned out, the trade show was a complete waste of time and money. We stood on our own two feet, similarly, chained to a wall you might say, for three days in a freezing and drafty part of the exhibition floor, collecting business cards and greeting hundreds of attendees.

Clinique

One Friday evening at about 6:00 pm, we received an email from the Executive Director of Global Marketing at Clinique, the famed cosmetic company. The email said:

"We would like to meet with Kim Parker to discuss a possible partnership between the Kim Parker brand and Clinique. We feel that both our brands have integrity. We have been following your career and your brand for years," the Director said. "Your design book has a lot of wear since everyone in the company has seen it, including the President of Estee Lauder."

Days later, we were scheduled for a meeting with the Vice President of Global Marketing, Executive Director and the Design Director at Clinique.

The corporate office for Clinique was located on Fifth Avenue right beside the old FAO Schwartz location and directly across from the elegant Plaza Hotel. It was a perfect late summer's day in New York City. We carried my black portfolio case full of hand painted silks and paper textile designs to share with them as per their request.

There was an amazing view from that high perch off the 37th floor, overlooking the lushness of Central Park. There were so many beautiful church spires and tops of buildings with fabulous gargoyles that I had never seen in all of the years we'd lived in the city. You could actually see all the way to the George Washington Bridge from there. The views were just spectacular.

It had been some time since I had returned to the corporate world. I was suddenly brought back to my early twenties when the young receptionist greeted me there with her cheerful smile. I had once sat behind a shiny reception desk like that too, right after college, a girl who had absolutely no idea where her life in New York City would take her.

Now I was seated in the waiting room about to meet with the Marketing VP at Clinique to discuss a potential "Kim Parker for Clinique" line of branded cosmetics that would feature my floral designs on them for worldwide distribution.

The VP of Global Marketing, the Executive Director, and Design Director greeted us kindly upon arrival. Felipe and I were escorted into a large office space with an equally stunning view of Manhattan. The VP was tall and dressed entirely in shiny black satin from head to toe, blouse, skirt and shoes, and jet-black hair. (For some reason I instantly envisioned a raven.) We all shook hands and sat down at her conference room table.

"We have been following your career for years," she said warmly to me. Taking my Abrams design book out and placing it upon the table before me, she told me, "I apologize for the condition of your book. It has been in everyone's hands here at Clinique. We are all blown away by your beautiful work. We believe that your brand and ours have equity, are both all about beauty, integrity and have a similar organic quality," she said. Then she laid out an entire global marketing campaign Clinique proposed to do, a "Kim Parker for Clinique" designer collaboration consisting of a line of cosmetics with both of our logos side by side on every product, that Clinique would distribute in 152 countries. "The collection will feature your floral designs on anything from lipsticks to cosmetic cases. You will be featured on the cover of our Clinique magazine. We will showcase any product you like from your designer collections including your art and design book on the inside of the magazine."

"We want you to tell your story, Kim. We think your story is exciting and very uniquely compelling. We see you as a quintessential New Yorker," she said. "By telling your story alongside your line of cosmetics, we feel it will give more dimension to this program." She went on to say that they had connections to all of the top fashion magazines and retailers worldwide. They would run articles or ads for my cosmetics line in Vogue, ELLE etc. She also suggested that I make personal appearances at department stores to promote the new collection. "Customers really like that," she said.

I listened as she spoke about the entire Kim Parker proposal. I was excited by this potential collaboration with Clinique. I opened my portfolio cases on the conference room table to show them the large archive of hand painted textile designs we would be able to select from. I brought along both my floral silk and paper textiles. The Design Director said to me enthusiastically, "These are so beautiful. Just so you know Kim, we can successfully duplicate any watercolor effect now with digital printing. We can capture all of the wonderful nuances of color and technique in your work. Any of these silk designs you are showing us here would work well for the new product line."

Everyone looked eagerly at each design as I went through the motions of carefully displaying them for about an hour. When the meeting ended, two hours later, Felipe and I were filled with hope and excitement. It seemed a bit odd to me however, that there was no mention whatsoever all throughout the two- hour meeting of a contract.

How could a huge company like Clinique not have even mentioned a contract, or royalty I wondered? If my products were to be distributed around the world, logically, we would need a contract. What royalties would they be offering for this global program?

I kept quiet about this until it was time to say goodbye. "When you have the contract," I said, "we will of course need time to pass it on to our attorney for proper review before any of the creative work begins." The VP turned slightly white, looking like she had seen a ghost. She was clearly caught off guard. It seemed very strange to me that my mentioning a contract would result in an awkward silence. Such a huge designer collaboration at a global scale, and with an extensive marketing plan would surely require a contract.

At the door we were generously handed two little bags full of lovely Clinique products as a parting gift. Then politely we all said our goodbyes.

"We will send you a contract," she said with slight hesitance, "but this could potentially hold things up, and time is of the essence. I worry that it could take some time to move it through our legal department."

After leaving the building, Felipe and I walked across Fifth Avenue with my print cases into Central Park. It was a beautiful, late summer's day. We were holding hands and feeling happy in our beloved city, sitting on a park bench all dressed up, and recapping our two-hour meeting.

I will end this New York story here. I can only say that like many, it held an air of mystery. I was told, a month later that they had to put the program "on hold." No explanation followed. My father, who had spent much of his corporate life in Manhattan, as Market Research Director for top companies on Park Avenue such as Bristol Meyers, Colgate, Lever Brothers and Cunard, found this totally "insane" that such a hugely wealthy company had not mentioned anything about a contract or compensation for such a huge program during the course of our meeting.

A year later however, on a summer's day, when we were walking down Fifth Avenue en route to another design meeting on 42nd Street, I saw a sign for a Clinique promotion outside of Lord & Taylor's Fifth Avenue department store. We popped inside to have a fast look at what was being promoted. Floral designs covering cosmetic cases and make up bags, and other products that bore a similarity to my own work (but in our opinions happily missed the mark) were on full display.

Paul Poiret: The King Of Fashion

When the Metropolitan Museum of Art held a retrospective called "The King of Fashion: Paul Poiret," Elle Décor magazine contacted me asking whether I could provide a quote for their upcoming feature story on this incredible fashion exhibition.

"This is Owen from Elle Décor Magazine. Is this Kim Parker?" the editor asked.

"Yes," I replied. "Elle Décor magazine is running a feature article on the upcoming exhibit on Paul Poiret at The Met. We wanted to get a few quotes from you since your work is clearly influenced by Poiret," he said.

I took a deep breath. "Owen," I said, (with some degree of embarrassment) "I am sorry to tell you this, but I don't know who Paul Poiret is."

Owen was silent at the other end of the phone. He asked me again, with an incredulous sound in his voice, whether I was sure I had never seen his work before. Again, I had to tell him that I was not familiar with Paul Poiret but deeply flattered that he had thought to quote me for such an important fashion exhibition.

When we got off the phone, I went immediately over to my computer to look up the name "Paul Poiret." I was instantly drawn to his opulent fashions and textile designs, many of which were floral and bold like my own. But it wasn't until I went to the actual exhibition at the Metropolitan Museum of Art that I realized why he had contacted me. Rugs and hand painted floral textile designs on silk as well as decorated hand painted perfume bottles and garments bore incredible likeness to my own work. Hand painted floral prints I had tucked away in my storage unit in a suitcase (that no one but Felipe had ever seen) were almost *exact* duplicates.

I stared at every display closely when walking this amazing fashion exhibition retrospective at The Met. I gazed in total awe at his opulent use of velvet and silk fabric. I identified with his love for using rich colors. I was stunned when noticing how close in style and hand our floral textile designs actually were. Images on exhibit of his richly colorful life in Paris in the early 1900s left me feeling somewhat haunted.

I bought all the books on Paul Poiret at the Metropolitan Museum gift shop my arms could carry home. My close friend in Paris sent me another large book on his work too that was out of print in French. He had a rich life as both a fine art painter as well as textile designer and became one of the world's first *"lifestyle designers."* His work could successfully dance on any number of surfaces in both the worlds of fashion and home decor, similar to my own.

Over the years, I had collected vintage coats, dresses and garments that I had found at local flea markets and thrift stores in Europe. Unknowingly, many of these vintage fashions were almost exact replicas of velvet coats and dresses that were featured in the actual exhibit and in the books purchased at the retrospective. Old black and white photographs of Poiret's black dog were even similar to our beloved dog Wendy, whose Munsterlander breed, we were told by our vet, was only found in Europe. I was also a huge fan of the painter Kees Van Dongen. I later discovered Paul Poiret and his wife Denise had a large Van Dongen hanging over their bed in Paris.

The more I kept reading about Paul Poiret's life the more I started finding uncanny commonalities between us. One such "coincidence" was an iron-gated doorway that I had been attracted to on Broadway for thirty years. Felipe and I must have passed that iron door one hundred times; arched and beautifully ornate with old, elegant iron work. Felipe would always stop and take pictures of me standing in front of it at my repeated request. I had told him for twenty years, "There is something about this iron doorway that I love. I just feel a connection with it." I later discovered, after looking through my many books on Poiret's life, that a photograph of the front door of his Parisian couture shop was eerily similar.

In my dresser drawer I had also collected (from numerous flea markets over the course of twenty years) old antique, brown colored perfume bottles that were decorated in delicately hand painted floral designs. I bought these old hand painted floral bottles simply because they were so pretty to my eyes. Here again, at the retrospective, unknowingly, were almost perfect replicas, painted in a similar hand, on full display from Poiret's "Rosine" perfume line.

At age fifteen I had the great fortune of going to Paris with my family for the very first time. Of course anyone who has ever gone to Paris has come away in awe from all of the beauty. But at age fifteen, on the way home in the plane I remember crying uncontrollably. My mother turned to me before take-off and said, "Kim, what's wrong? Why are you crying so much?" I could not speak. "I think I know why you are crying," she said, "It must be because you have never seen so much beauty in all of your life and you are deeply moved and don't want to leave. I feel the same way." I never forgot that moment. I quickly accepted her reasoning of my sadness as true. I am not sure however, in retrospect, that I was not reliving some past-life memory and experience.

I returned several times to the Poiret exhibition at the Metropolitan Museum of Art. Poiret was one of the greatest couturiers that had ever lived. I identified strongly with his passion for beauty, his courageous use of bold motifs, and love of floral designs in rich colors. Sadly however, after years of being exalted in France as the "King of Fashion" who lived a lavish Parisian life of parties and tremendous successes, he wound up destitute. The war had changed Europe and many successful businesses ultimately crashed. He was a painter first and foremost. He then became a fashion designer, who freed women from wearing a corset by designing dresses and coats that were generous in fabric, and lush in design. The interior of his Parisian shop resembled our own living room in New York City, with densely populated floral fabrics upholstered upon antiques with floral wallpapers to match.

I started to really wonder whether in a past life, I might have possibly been Paul Poiret? Why had Owen, a top editor at Elle Décor magazine contacted me that day, so sure that I knew who Poiret was? I knew I could not share these feelings with anyone but Felipe. But when I told Gil, my Buddhist healer, he responded:

"Kim, it is very possible, because you would have had to be famous in the art, fashion or design world in a *past* life for you to have this level of visibility and success that you now have in this life. It's called *cumulative karma*."

It would be difficult to explain how my floral textile designs that no one had ever seen before sitting quietly for years in my suitcases, bore an almost exact resemblance to designs featured in Paul Poiret's art books and at the Metropolitan Museum of Art's exhibition.

Realization

A dear Brazilian friend of mine, a fine journalist in New York, Wesley, (whom I had not seen for almost three decades) came to visit me one afternoon. He had (unknowingly) been following my career all those years. After our reunion he wrote:

"*Kim, someone has to say it, so it may as well be me. Yours is the kind of talent that can beautify anything that comes your way, and not just material things. Those who know of you are aware of this soulful quality. But to everyone else, your gifts are so evident to transpire through your creations. That's another way you touch and move people, and it's almost the same way your spirit does. It's a harsh world out there, so heaven knows, we all need to have people like you around. Hope you keep helping us dream of a better world, just by looking at your pieces. I am so proud of you. I know how hard you have worked. Your life is all about realization. It is really beautiful to s ee.*"

The word "*realization*" replayed in my mind for days afterward. Always on to the next creative project, living with a constant stream of inspired ideas and visions before me, I admit that it is hard to sometimes quietly reflect on the things that *have* been thankfully, *realized*. When does one truly feel *realized*? Is it when holding a book in your hands that chronicles your life? Is it when you receive an award in the industry for design achievements? Or a bestselling collection sells for years and has a timeless appeal? Or is it really, when you know you have followed your heart, your intuition, and courageously forged a creative life that has reached many.

All I know is ... that Wesley's kind words, during a time when things were a bit challenging, and when I was feeling disenchanted, gave me pause. I knew my path was anything but conventional. I knew that certain opportunities had oddly slipped away, while others had been *realized*. My head and heart were always full of dreams. Sometimes it felt like there were too many to realize in one lifetime.

Mikasa

Lifetime Brands is one of the largest tabletop companies in the United States. Their spacious and brightly lit showroom was on the corner of 26th Street, by Madison Square Park. From the start Henry, the Design Director at Mikasa, was very enthusiastic about our potential tabletop designer collaboration.

"Do you know how many designers approach our company wanting to be licensed each year?" he asked.

We went through hundreds of my original designs together so that he could see all of the dinnerware possibilities.

"I will need fifteen new dinnerware patterns from you, Kim. I will then take them to the president for consideration."

I was no newcomer to the dinnerware world. I'd designed collections for Block China, Sasaki, and Spode. Designing fifteen new dinnerware patterns however was a pretty hefty request, in just four weeks.

I certainly never had any shortage of creative ideas, but it would mean many hours of work without a guarantee of being signed on. I'd never worked that way before. No other dinnerware company had ever asked for that amount of design work prior to being offered a contract. I was already pretty much a veteran in the dinnerware industry.

I poured myself into the design process without coming up for air--creating fifteen, new dinnerware templates both floral and geometric over the course of one month. Some of these new designs had a bit of a Scandinavian look, while others were loosely rendered- florals. Most of the dinnerware world was solid white, with no color. Most people didn't want too much pattern on their plates. When I finished the thirty templates to show the president, we agreed to meet at their showroom.

At 41 Madison Avenue, in the conference room overlooking Madison Square Park, Henry put his hand firmly over the top of my designs, smiled and said:

"Kim, You have really gone above and beyond here. These are totally beautiful." Pulling the prints aside that he truly felt had the best chance of securing our potential designer collaboration and meeting the approval of the company president, he thanked me and told us he would be in touch in a week or two.

Many weeks went by and we had no idea what was going on. But finally, Henry called us with the good news and the green light. We would be signing on with Mikasa for a new tabletop and giftware licensing designer collaboration.

On opening night at 45 Madison Avenue in the Lifetime Brands showroom, my new porcelain dinnerware collections were launched. All of my floral patterns were produced with integrity. The event was catered with beautiful hors d'oeuvres, sparkling wine and champagne and lively exchanges with industry editors, buyers and salespeople and a showroom buzzing with positive energy.

French Fashion designer Catherine Malandrino attended. She and I had known each other from years back. We had not seen one another for a long time. Prior to the launch of her namesake brand in the fashion world, she was the head designer at Diane Von Furstenberg in the West Village. It was there where she used to buy my silk designs for Diane's dress line. We embraced warmly at this Madison Avenue opening.

"Kim," Catherine said, (when we were alone) "you were very smart to stick with what you do best. You have a distinctive look in the industry that is really recognizable, and I am so happy for you. Your new tableware collections look great."

It was another magical dinnerware launch. Macy's again committed to carrying three of my new dinnerware collections on opening night, which then led the way for other major US retailers to follow their lead with the same confidence.

Farewell to a New York Treasure

New York Central, my favorite art supply store in the city announced it would be closing its doors after a mere one hundred and ten years. It opened in 1905. It was considered one of the world's oldest and best-known art supply stores in the country. Pop artists Andy Warhol and Roy Lichtenstein, as well as painters Willem De Kooning and Jean Michel Basquiat all bought their materials there.

Unlike its chain store competitors, New York Central Art Supply had just one location in the city, offering their loyal clientele an old-world type of personal, one on one service. It was the Patelson Music store of the art supply world. It was one of the few art stores left in the city with a soul. Many of the artists working behind the counters were knowledgeable and talented themselves. They were able to recommend all kinds of useful information to anyone coming through the door. If you had a question about a paper quality, or wanted to know what the finest type of acrylic or oil paint was or which type of brush to use for this or that affect, the answers would come easily and pleasantly from their employees.

So for more than three decades I made many pilgrimages to this neighborhood art supply store, carting off large sheets of watercolor paper, silk dyes, gouache paint and all kinds of other art supplies back to my home studio. I forged friendships with the faithful employees who always greeted both of my beloved dogs Maggie and Wendy with yummy treats and affection.

I must admit that when I read that the building had been sold, I felt extremely sickened. I couldn't imagine how it would feel to walk past that storefront on Third Avenue once boarded up, never to make those inspired city walks again. Artist friends all seemed to be feeling it too.

So with a bit of a lump in our throats, on a hot summer's day, Felipe, Wendy and I headed there for the very last time. It would soon shut its doors forever. When I got upstairs to the paper department, greeted by my longtime employee friend Caitlin behind the counter, who had worked there for most of her adult life, loved our dogs, and never had anything but kind words, we just looked at each other. We stretched our arms across the large wooden countertop between us, and with tears in our eyes, held hands silently. We knew an era was ending.

I decided to buy two large packets of my favorite watercolor paper, a specific type I could not find anyplace else in the city, as a final purchase. She took the two large heavy-duty packets down from off the old wooden shelving units, placed them on the counter and asked as she had always:

"Do you want them rolled or flat packed in cardboard, Kim?"

"Cardboard is fine, thanks, Caitlin," I told her. I watched as she prepared the paper for me to cart home, creating a special handle to make it easier. These were precious rituals in my New York City life of thirty-three years.

Placing my credit card down on the counter to pay for these two large packs of beautiful Saunders paper, she pushed the card back in my direction. Saying nothing, just looking at me with eyes that read:

"Please, put it away. This is my parting gift to you,"

I asked, "Are you sure?" She nodded. We hugged each other one more time before leaving. As Felipe and I made our way down the steep steps leading to the front entrance of the store, I spontaneously took a moment to thank all of the employees congregated by the front register. Everyone in the store started clapping in appreciation of their fine services to the artistic community.

Felipe, Wendy and I hit the hot city streets walking away with generous packets of my favorite paper. "I cannot believe you just got all of this beautiful paper for free," Felipe said. "That was for thirty years of patronage, honey." Felipe carried it home carefully under his arm as he had always done, while I walked Wendy.

When I got home, I called Caitlin at the store. "What is your favorite color?" I asked. "Green," the Irish girl appropriately replied. An hour later back out in the 100 degree heat of the city streets, I made my last, faithful East Village walk to that beloved art supply store - with a green floral embroidered pillow from my collection, wrapped in tissue paper.

The Psychic in Hell's Kitchen

One of New York City's best-kept secrets is Louise, an adorable, Gemini mystic and psychic who was recommended to me by my Buddhist healer Gil. Every four years I would find myself in her darkly lit apartment in the neighborhood of Hell's Kitchen. She knew a lot about astrology, numerology and mythology. Information poured out of her in a very stream of consciousness manner. Her psychic sessions were always taped on a cassette so that when you got home, you could play it all back again. She had accurately predicted many things over twenty years.

"You will have a great deal of success in London," she told me, long before I did.

"You and your husband will be business partners," which a few years later became true too. But one thing she said really impacted me.

"In all of my years as a psychic, I have waited to meet someone who was married to their *twin soul*. You and your husband are twin souls," she said, "You're both a gift to the world."

When I got home that afternoon I read up on the meaning of "twin souls." I had only read once before about it, in one of Shirley MacLaine's books.

The dictionary defines "twin souls" as: "The moment your soul was created, it possessed, male-female, yin-yang polarity and energy. God's love for you made sure that these two complementary forms of consciousness, both masculine and feminine, would be bound together throughout eternity. The twin halves of two souls have been called twin souls, twin vibrations. In other words, you only have one twin soul, the other half of your soul in the entire Universe who vibrates at the same frequency of light that you do."

Plato even said of twin souls, "*And one of them meets with his other half, the actual half of himself, the pair are lost in an amazement of love and friendship and intimacy, and one will not be without the other's sight, even for a moment.*" Well that was certainly true.

Louise also said that we would be buying a country home in Stone Ridge, New York, a place I had never heard of before. She had no idea where Stone Ridge was herself. After months of having given up on looking for a house in the Catskills, my mother called and asked:

"Are you two still trying to find a house upstate or have you given up? Maybe you're on the wrong side of the Catskills. You two should try looking for a house in Stone Ridge. My cousin actually owns a B&B there."

That day I connected with her cousin, who then swiftly put me in touch with a realtor. After seeing just two homes, we purchased a charming 1930's farmhouse in Stone Ridge.

The very last time I spoke with Louise, Felipe and I were in the process of trying to find a new apartment in Manhattan. We were in a bit of a crisis.

"Are we going to stay in New York City?" I asked her frantically, "Or are we going to move someplace else?"

"No honey," Louise said, "You will be staying here, but you will have to edit. Saturn is over your Moon right now asking you to cut away what you don't need anymore. You'll have to lighten your load a lot. You will need to part ways with what is no longer necessary, but you'll be fine."

We had lived in our Gramercy Park brownstone apartment on East 18th Street for fifteen happy years, on a landmark block with blossoming trees and a back courtyard that provided us with lush greenery, peace and an amazing array of birds. We had cardinals, blue jays, finches, pigeons, hawks, and squirrels that would come regularly to our windowsill where I had always left slices of cut apple and peanut butter.

Our apartment interior would be featured in several lifestyle magazines such as: Country Living, The London Guardian, Living Etc., the New York Post Page Six, and Elle Decoration UK. After fifteen years living comfortably in this enchanted space and paying a rent that was affordable, our landlords informed us that they had to move their daughter into our apartment as soon as our lease was up. It was January and our lease would be up in early June. We had not moved inside Manhattan for fifteen years. We had absolutely no idea what awaited us in terms of the challenges of finding a new apartment in New York City, one we could afford.

This news came at an extremely difficult time. My stepfather Ernie was extremely ill in a hospital. One prepaid travel commitment was cancelled. We had hoped to find another brownstone apartment, like the one we currently occupied, to maintain the feeling of a charming and elegant interior, but the New York City rental market had drastically changed over the past fifteen years. Such an apartment at the rent we'd been paying, was an anachronism.

Landlords and management companies now expected three years worth of tax returns showing 40X the monthly rent, credit scores, bank account balances, etc. If you could get a letter from a landlord stating you'd been a good tenant that was also good to have.

The apartments that we were taken to in our neighborhood of Gramercy Park, where we had hoped to remain since our doctors, vets, and community were important to keep, were visuals I hope will one day be erased from my memory. Most were no larger than a jail cell. We had been living in a real estate bubble for fifteen years without knowing it.

Our landlords were kind not to have raised our rent too much over fifteen years. They were both therapists whose practices were right below our living room and bedroom, so we agreed to live like Anne Frank during daylight hours to honor their need for quiet. We didn't play our stereo. I didn't practice my flute until after 7pm. We had sacrifices to make to maintain a lower rent.

In truth, I grew to like the peace they had required we keep. Being that I was an artist whose days were largely spent quietly writing or painting, it worked out well, even though it slightly prohibited me from picking up my flute spontaneously in the middle of the day when I felt inspired.

In the beginning of this real estate odyssey, we went far uptown to the top of Manhattan to Washington Heights, where one apartment faced the George Washington Bridge. At night that majestic bridge was pretty dramatically lit. The apartment was actually one of the nicer and more spacious places we ultimately had seen over five months of searching. Felipe and I walked through that unfamiliar neighborhood, but after thirty years living downtown, it felt like we'd moved to Mars.

It would take us a long time to get back to our beloved zip code by subway train downtown. This charming Hispanic neighborhood, although slowly trying to transition into a more gentrified area, was still far from it. There was a sweet community feeling, similar to one that you might get in parts of Queens amid certain Latin cultures. The smell of fried fish and plantains, culinary specialties that were Cuban, Dominican and Puerto Rican seemed to be readily available even on the street. The only thing I recognized was Citibank. Bodegas with fresh fruits and vegetables were situated here and there. It was a nice place to come and visit and explore, but we both felt strongly that it could not be our home.

We went to the bottom of Manhattan too, to Art Deco buildings off of Wall Street that again were tight spaces with views of steel buildings out every window- a real reminder for me of the hard aspect of city life. After looking at an inner courtyard with birds and trees for fifteen years, I couldn't make that change. At Battery Park City we saw just one apartment that faced the cheerful image of the Holocaust Museum, a daily reminder of one of history's darkest periods.

Felipe had me sold for a while on the Upper West Side. We both had a very good feeling about it given we'd both spent our earlier years roaming the streets there. The Beaux Arts Mansions off of Riverside Drive, or any brownstones nearer to Central Park we thought would be ideal given we had a dog, wanting to stay as close as we could to greenery. What I could not have anticipated was how the large majority of these apartments were so poorly managed, with rodents, cat pee stench, roaches, and antiquated kitchen appliances that looked like they had not been updated since the 1970's. These interiors were in serious need of TLC and fixing up, many of them filthy. Many brownstone apartments once spacious in size were now divided down the middle with a wall that not only looked completely unnatural, making it difficult to fit a bed on the one said of the wall designated "bedroom." Most bedrooms couldn't even accommodate a dresser. It was totally depressing.

We wound up looking at 158 apartments in six exhausting months. We worked with many different real estate agents, most of whom were young twenty something year old kids whose patience wore thin after showing just three apartments. They wanted their generous commissions easily, and with the turnover in New York, they probably got it. I wasn't good at making swift decisions about what to call "home." I knew it would speak to me when I walked in, like our Gramercy Park brownstone did.

After viewing about ninety apartments I was already in a state of compete and total exhaustion, praying for a bedroom with just a tree out the window, a place I could find deep repose and die in. I was verging on complete physical and emotional collapse. In one instance I actually broke down crying in front of the realtor when sitting on a sofa inside of an apartment he was showing me.

There were other serious issues too such as bedbug reports and infestations. I had home furnishings inventory we kept in bins that needed to be protected. We sold these goods on our website, so that wasn't going to cut it. Real estate agents tried making it sound like it was no big deal if a building had a bedbug history. We did our own due diligence throughout that time, looking up building addresses on a city Bed Bug website that provided that information.

In our own beloved Gramercy neighborhood, apparently "the most desirable zip code" in New York City, we were told by realtors, the spaces were so small that you had to be careful not to walk in the door too fast or you'd fall out the front window.

One of the realtors, a lovely woman in her seventies who occupied a large one bedroom apartment in Chelsea for the past forty-five years, Betty, after seeing our brownstone interior featured in my Abrams design book said,

"Honey, I can understand why this has been so hard for you. I feel sorry for you guys. Nothing like this exists anymore in New York City. You've become accustomed to living in a gracious space and paying rent that is a thing of the past. I've occupied my own apartment for forty-five years, in Chelsea, and if this was happening to me right now, I would never be able to afford living in New York City again. I don't know where I'd go."

I loved working with her during our odyssey. She accompanied me to a number of Upper West Side and Harlem apartments and in one instance said to the landlord who was showing me his newly renovated tiny one bedroom:

"Oh no honey! This won't do at all! Where the heck are the closets? A woman cannot live without closets! Let's get out of here!"

Her good humor brought levity to this endless process and we laughed together sometimes at the absurdly horrible conditions of many of the apartments we were seeing. Sometimes we had to sit down and have a drink afterward for comic relief.

We spent many days in numerous Brooklyn neighborhoods too such as Park Slope, Brooklyn Heights, Clinton Hill because we were trying to recapture that beautiful brownstone feeling which in fact we succeeded in doing in Park Slope.

Two blocks from Prospect Park, about four months into this journey, a lovely brownstone apartment surfaced at an affordable rent in a beautiful neighborhood. I could totally envision us living there. I heard birds out my bedroom window, which pleased me. My problem with Brooklyn was that I was not a "straphanger." I didn't ride the subway, so my only way back into Manhattan would be by rental car or bus, which I didn't think was a great situation given we would be doing a lot of business inside the city.

It was ultimately Felipe, the kid who grew up on Riverside Drive in Manhattan, and born on Christopher Street, who to my surprise, at the very last moment before signing the lease for this Brooklyn brownstone apartment, and paying our "good faith deposit", went into a state of sudden panic.

"I am so sorry honey. I cannot do it," he said frantically, trying to catch his breath. "My DNA is in Manhattan!"

It was rare to see him in this type of panic mode, but I was not about to force him to live in a zip code he was not OK with.

Many of our dearest friends lived in beautiful Brooklyn, including my nephew. Felipe and I loved Brooklyn in truth. We often spent time with our beloved dog Wendy in Prospect Park and in springtime, in the Botanical Gardens. We even had our second date there. But it's true that New Yorkers really dig their feet into the zip codes they have occupied for many years forming close identities and forging meaningful connections to doctors and friends within their communities. Ours was Gramercy Park and the Flatiron District for more than thirty years.

Queens was out. I had already lived there for five years with my first husband right out of college. I knew what to expect. Although one spacious apartment did present itself in Queens during our odyssey, with charming old arched doorways and classic bookshelves lining the walls of the living room, wooden floors and high ceilings too, we simply couldn't imagine life there. All of my father's relatives and all four of my beloved grandparents had lived in Queens when I was growing up. For me, living in a zip code surrounded by the memories of so many deceased, beloved relatives as well as an ex husband, was just too emotionally heavy.

June was now approaching and our lease would soon be up. A trip to Nantucket we had planned sadly fell away during this process– a short trip we had made a year in advance that we were looking forward to. There was simply no time to go there while we were desperate to settle into a new apartment in Manhattan. The clock was ticking. I literally was sick. The search for a home was taking a very heavy physical and emotional toll on me. Felipe was worried about my health.

During all of that, I was packing up our entire apartment of fifteen years, and exhaustive chore. Fifteen years of accumulating all kinds of things tightly packed into every crevice of our humble abode now needed to be cut away.

My psychic was right about "editing." I sold tons of things to neighbors and donated books to The Strand. By the end of four and a half months we had seen a total of 158 apartments. My stepfather Ernie, aptly compared the toll moving took upon people, to death.

Still days before the expiration of our brownstone's lease, we worried about where we would wind up living, when at the buzzer, in June, in a state of exhaustion and desperation, I asked Felipe if he would could revisit one tall brick building complex right down the block from where we had been living in Gramercy Park for fifteen years, a community called Stuyvesant Town. We had frequented its grounds with our dogs for many years. Nature was everywhere there. It had a park-like atmosphere that we enjoyed walking through. The brick buildings were not aesthetically pretty, and resembled lower income housing.

I called the leasing office one more time to see whether there were any apartments available for rent. Sure enough, just a few days before our lease was due to expire, and our landlord worried that we might not vacate it on time; an apartment presented itself.

From the very start of this apartment search, I had envisioned trees out my windows with a southern exposure. The majority of apartments on the Upper East and Upper West sides faced either other buildings or dark airshafts out their windows, which I knew I could not bare. My eyes and spirit craved light, greenery and peace. I must have meditated every single day for the six-month duration for trees out my windows. Felipe and I crossed Central Park on foot during the bitter cold days of January to the brutally hot days of early summer, from East Side to West Side, looking at all possibilities.

This entire process made me well aware of the importance of visualization. No matter how defeated or deflated I had felt at any given moment, somehow, I never lost the image in my head of having trees and southern light out my windows. I held that visual strongly in my mind the whole way through. I just believed that there had to be an apartment someplace in Manhattan where I could hear a bird singing, or see a tree out my window.

A Unique Manhattan Enclave

Our new apartment in Stuyvesant Town offered a much different type of New York City lifestyle than all the other apartments we occupied over the course of thirty years.

Stuyvesant Town was a unique community full of Sycamore trees, colorful flowers, a central fountain, clean benches to sit on, chess tables, playgrounds, a café, outdoor movies, a Sunday farmer's market, basketball courts and a beautiful open lawn for sunbathing and picnicking.

An ethnically diverse community inside the city, it accommodated college students, young couples embarking on parenthood, and old timers who'd been nestled there quite affordably, for more than forty years. Many paid practically no rent by current New York City standards.

Not long after we settled in, we were invited to sit at the outdoor chess tables for a neighbor's delicious homemade pizza party. On the big open lawn, classical and jazz concerts were given weekly. On Wednesday evenings throughout the summer, there were outdoor movies, and every weekend until November, a fresh farmer's market. By Christmas, lights were festively and gracefully strewn in tall trees, and a large Menorah and Christmas tree standing centrally on the Oval lawn.

When we moved into our new apartment, with windows facing South and full of light as I had dreamed, branches of trees with squirrels and jays upon them, I was amazed after 158 apartments, that we had found everything we meditated on. Out front, young boys were playing basketball on a large court. This was *urban life* at its best.

Listening to these young boys bouncing basketballs throughout the day, shouting the way kids do passing a ball, Felipe pointed out, "It is pure West Side Story." Any connection to Leonard Bernstein was magical. This urban vibe really sealed the deal for us.

It took no time to forge meaningful friendships with people from different cultural backgrounds. For fifteen years, on our old and elegant brownstone block on East 18th Street, things were not quite this way.

What I have experienced in all of the neighborhoods I have lived in over the past thirty years in Manhattan, is that New Yorkers like a certain degree of privacy and anonymity. They will superficially greet one another if they happen to be leaving at the same time. There is a kind of social boundary respectfully kept, an unspoken rule of New York City life.

In Stuyvesant Town this rule did not apply somehow. Everyone stopped to talk. The sense of community was strong. It reminded me of the suburban neighborhood on Long Island that I had grown up in.

The tall brick buildings were not exactly Beaux Arts Mansions aesthetically speaking. Felipe affectionately referred to them as "a Roman fortress." In the morning there was a rosy glow at sunrise, similar to the clay-colored cast of Rome. Framed by beautiful tall Sycamore trees forming graceful archways (the way I remember many roads in the French countryside did) we felt a different type of enchantment and connection to the seasons. Felipe also liked referring affectionately to the portal of Sycamore trees as "The Bois de Boulogne."

Manuel, a groundskeeper in Stuyvesant Town, rolling his big pails and rakes around, asked me one morning, "Can you smell the soil?" He points to a red Tail Hawk perching on one of the lower branches of a tall tree. I see this huge wild bird waiting to prey upon one unlucky squirrel or pigeon. We watch together quietly. "Take a picture," he says with a smile. Two old ladies speaking Spanish pass by. I say, "Look ladies! Do you see the hawk?" "That's the son!" one of them says excitedly. "We've seen the father!"

I continue my walk, through the sweetness of a November rain that softens the ground pushing up the fresh scent of dampened earth. I remind myself that I am in New York City not in the middle of some rural wooded area. Two, author -women acquaintances jog by and say hello. They have both lived here for more than twenty years in this enclave and tell me, "People look at the tall brick buildings and think it's ugly, and we're glad they don't know how beautiful it *really* is."

At night, no matter what hour, when I look out my bedroom window, I see hundreds of living room lights illuminated like fireflies. If for a moment I ever feel alone, I know that I am not.

"You Are The Flower Market"

I head towards the 14th Street Union Square farmer's market, a fifteen-minute walk that I never take for granted. I have thankfully learned how to "transport" myself to any part of the world when I am walking. A fallen leaf can trigger a memory of the woods in Belgium. I have traveled and lived abroad, and collaborated with companies from overseas. I have had the good fortune of traveling to Australia, New Zealand, Tahiti, Samoa, Tonga and the Cook Islands. I have been numerous times to Brazil and vacationed on most of the Caribbean islands. My father took us to Haiti in the 1970s where we witnessed real suffering and poverty but were profoundly moved by the beautiful spirit of the Haitian people. I worked on a cruise ship that sailed to Alaska and I traveled across a good portion of Europe when living in Belgium.

My morning walks across 14th Street allow me to observe the richness of New York City life. I see plenty that I wish I could change. Many are in need of money and emotional support. I say hi to Rashid, in his little truck faithfully parked along 2nd Avenue where he sells Middle Eastern food to put his daughter through college. The old, Russian souvenirs and war artifacts store is finally boarded up. I held a secret affection for that old, jumbled storefront whose window display never changed in thirty years. Felipe bought me a pair of Finift porcelain earrings there during our first year of marriage. Our old Irish friend Jim used to say when a store had closed that it made him sad because it "was the end of a dream."

Union Square has been the joyful hub and heart of my urban life. It is where Felipe once lovingly called out my name when we met up coincidentally, shortly after we had first met at the Halloween party. It is where we found our darling and beloved dog Wendy, who was up for adoption one brutally hot summer's day. I cannot count how many times this outdoor market lifted my spirits, simply by walking through her abundance of flowers and fresh smelling vegetables and breads. My long-time friend Michaela poetically said, when she thought we might be leaving the neighborhood after three decades:

"You can't go, Kim. You *are* the Flower Market."

We could have easily enjoyed walking through the elegant streets of Brooklyn brownstones and gardens had we not found our place in Stuyvesant Town. I could have enjoyed apple blossoming trees bursting with joy each spring in Prospect Park. I am all for beauty. But I have always slightly preferred when things were *not perfect*.

The East Village, also affectionately known as "Loisada" or the Lower East Side, still held onto its charming edginess. Hispanic older men sitting on milk crates playing the guitar with their backs set against the Projects felt "real" to me. There were no chain stores for blocks, only humble businesses situated along Avenues B and C; each door with a friendly personalized service from hair salons, cheese shops and small cafes to Chinese tailors. Morning walks to the gym down 12th Street towards Union Square taught me to find my step with full presence. No morning walk was ever the same. The quiet of the morning down tree-lined streets, past schoolyards and small gardens tucked between tenements, held all the poetry of any other place in the world.

The Robin's Song

One of the things that made it difficult to walk away from our charmed-brownstone life of fifteen years in Gramercy Park on East 18th Street was that a robin would sing her heart out early in the morning. I would often lay awake listening in awe. At the age of eight, my parents felt that it was time for me to join the family quartet, and asked, "What instrument would you like to play?" my mother tells me that I replied, "The flute, because it sounds like a bird."

As I was leaving our brownstone life for the last time with Wendy our beloved dog, making my way with a few heavy satchels under my arms towards our new apartment down the street in Stuyvesant Town, I was sad to leave the robin's song behind. Perhaps it was a replay of having walked away from my own song, my musical past.

Wendy seemed reluctant when walking towards our new address. She kept pulling me back towards the front stoop. This was her first New York City home. We had often walked with her through the shady grounds of Stuyvesant Town on hot summer days. It was always a lot cooler there beneath the trees and she had squirrels to chase. But Wendy knew everything. Certainly having watched me box an entire apartment for a period of six months while living amid a warehouse aesthetic, was enough evidence for her eyes that things were changing.

The brownstone was my laboratory aesthetically. Magazines came to profile me there. It had beautiful, old bones and brick walls, and large windows that faced an inner courtyard full of singing birds. I quietly painted hundreds of textile designs at my dining room table for fifteen years there.

While living in our brownstone apartment, I sometimes played my flute during the few hours that our landlords were not in session with their therapy clients. Most of the time it was just improvising to Brazilian jazz. However, we had to respect the owner's request for silence, which kept me away from my instrument.

As Wendy and I made our way towards our new Stuyvesant Town address, pulling me back towards our old domain, sensing then that all we had come to comfortably know as "home" for fifteen years was now transitioning, I have to admit, I too was warding off my attachment to our cozy life. I gently pulled her forward. "Come on Wendy, we have a *new* home now. Just come with mama," I said with as much cheer as I could muster.

Quite miraculously, the very first morning in our new Stuyvesant Town apartment, at about 3:00am, a robin was singing its heart outside our bedroom window. The tall brick buildings were like her concert hall, bringing even greater resonance to her beautiful heartfelt song. With tears in my eyes I took Felipe's hand. "Listen honey. Can you believe it?" The music had followed us, a harbinger of good things to come.

Playing for Jean Pierre Rampal

When I was thirteen years old, my father, a very talented violinist, who supported his family by commuting into Manhattan each day and working in the corporate world, came home with The New York Times in his hands.

"Kimmie, how would you like to audition to play for the great Jean Pierre Rampal?" he asked. He showed me an advertisement he had torn out of the NY Times with a photo of Jean Pierre Rampal, world- renowned flutist. It read: "Mr. Rampal gives a Masterclass to Ten Flutists at the 92 Street Y, in New York City." Below it were instructions on how to submit a tape for the audition.

Rampal was considered one of the greatest flutists in the world. He had recorded pretty much everything written for the instrument. He taught at the Conservatoire in Paris. My parents bought me all of his flute recordings in the 1970's. I became extremely familiar with most of the flute repertoire through his very French interpretations. He played with a rich and warm tone that I loved, and although he often played most things too fast in my opinion, his masterful technique and command of the instrument were awe-inspiring.

When my father showed me the New York Times announcement, I felt instantly nervous. He was sure that we could put together quickly a quality audition tape and submit it. The rules stated that you had to be older than eighteen to enter. I was just thirteen at the time. I prepared a good quality cassette in our living room with my mother accompanying me at the piano, playing works of Bach, Quantz, and Debussy.

About two months later I received a phone call from the Director at the 92 Street Y in charge of this Masterclass event.

"Kim Parker has been selected by Monsieur Rampal to be one of ten flutists to participate in a masterclass at the 92nd Street Y in New York City," she said.

I remember that moment so vividly. I was leaning up against our refrigerator door, sliding straight down to the floor, incredulously, when I heard that I had been chosen. No one was home.

"Monsieur Rampal has requested that you prepare the Quantz G Major Flute Concerto for him," the Director said. When my father came home from work later that evening, he called them back just to confirm that I had gotten the message straight.

The next two months were spent practicing the Quantz G Major Flute Concerto. My father patiently coached me, while my mother accompanied me on the piano. Joachim Quantz was very much like Mozart. This G Major concerto had a crisp and lively tempo. I was asked to prepare it in its entirety.

Several weeks later, the day of this master class arrived. I really was perhaps too young to understand what was about to happen. I had never performed in a masterclass before, and I didn't really know that a masterclass was basically going to be a private lesson before a live audience. I had never even thought to ask.

Inside Kaufmann Hall the masterclass would also be televised on PBS. In the green room backstage, I heard the other nine flute players who were selected too, warming up. All of them were a lot older than me. It seemed that everyone was doing their best to impress and out shine each other, playing flashy technical runs on the instrument. I waited for my name to be called, my heart beating fast.

Each flutist was given thirty minutes on stage with Monsieur Rampal. Walking out under very bright lights to a full house, and applause, I walked in the direction of this renowned flutist. Wearing a blue jeans jumper and red flannel shirt, clogs and tights (not exactly a dressy choice of attire I admit), Rampal instantly greeted me warmly, putting his arm around me endearingly, and asking in his thick French accent, "ça va?" "Oui, ça va bien, merci, " I replied in my junior high school French.

"Quel age avez- vous?" he asked. (How old are you?)

Looking up in fear I replied, "J'ai treize ans..." (knowing that I was actually not even allowed to enter the competition unless I was seventeen.) Monsieur Rampal paused. He turned to the audience and said jokingly in English,

"My God, when I was thirteen, I couldn't even blow my nose!" Everyone laughed.

I was introduced to my accompanist, a pianist with whom I had never played. He nodded at me and soon started playing the introduction to the Quantz G Major Flute Concerto, the "Tutti" of the first movement.

I managed to play straight through the first page of the opening movement confidently. Then Monsiuer Rampal stopped me. He noticed that I had developed what he called in his thick French accent "a fixation" – a habit of playing middle D with my first finger down, which was technically incorrect. I had to correct this old "fixation"(habit) that I had developed for years, in just thirty minutes before a live audience. Not so easy.

The lesson continued. We moved on to the second slower, more lyrical Adagio movement of the concerto. He played it for me with a beautiful tone on a flute made of solid gold. His warm, French voluptuous sound inspired my young ears and heart. By the end of the class, once again with his arm around my back, he said affectionately after I finished playing, "Ahh voila Kim, tres bien, merci, brava! "

Monsiuer Rampal returned yet again to the 92 Street Y to give another masterclass to ten lucky flutists the following year. My father convinced me to again submit another audition tape, and again I was selected to play for him the following year out of hundreds of applicants I was told.

I played the Bach E Minor Flute Sonata, a staple in the flute repertoire. I was not as nervous the second year. I knew what to expect this time around at age fourteen. It was an honor to play for him again, adding to the richness of an earlier musical career.

Rampal teaching Kim Parker - Masterclass at the 92nd Street Y

A Sabbatical at Oberlin

Throughout high school and during my four years of flute study at Oberlin Conservatory of Music, I was steadily preparing for an orchestral career with my professor, Robert Willoughby. The solo flute repertoire was beautiful, however limited in comparison to the richness of the orchestral flute repertoire.

Much to my delight and surprise one semester, flutist Karl Kraber arrived as a sabbatical replacement for Mr. Willoughby. Karl had studied with both Jean Pierre Rampal and the great Marcel Moyse. He had also performed with both the New York Philharmonic and Boston Pops. He too played in the French School style.

It was immediately evident to me in my first lesson with him that I was going to love studying with him, which I did. I felt inspired again. He was instantly supportive and wonderfully appreciative of my playing. Similar to my favorite teacher Harold Bennett's approach, Karl played his flute in an expressive and warm French style. He assigned me principal flute orchestral parts for pieces he felt I would play well, such as Ravel's "Tombeau de Couperin." He also encouraged me to take an audition for the Fellowship orchestra at Tanglewood; an older graduate orchestral, musical program there that was highly competitive.

Typically, only three flutists would be accepted into the Tanglewood Fellowship Orchestra. Since entering college, this would be my very first professional orchestral audition held in Cleveland at the Cleveland Institute of Music. Preparing a long list of the standard, difficult solo flute orchestral excerpts, I prepared what was expected for the judges. These were orchestral excerpts I had worked on for years. The list was extensive and demanding- which included the works of Prokofiev, Strauss, Berlioz, Beethoven, and Stravinsky, to name a few. I entered the small room at the Cleveland Institute of Music and greeted the judges who would decide which flute excerpts they wanted to hear. I had no idea, out of a long list of orchestral excerpts which ones I'd been asked to play on the spot.

One of the judges, a conductor, asked me to begin with the flute solo from the Beethoven Leonore Overture No. 3. This brilliant flute solo begins with a quick opening run, a flourish of notes leading into the highest register of the instrument followed by fast finger and tonguing work highlighting the theme. I knew this excerpt quite well and I felt confident in my preparation. I played through the solo cleanly and swiftly and "note perfectly" for the judges. After I finished the conductor said:

"I have to tell you, I have never heard that solo played that fast and cleanly in all my life. May I ask you something?"

"Yes, of course, "I replied.

"Are you familiar with this orchestral work?"

"Yes, I am," I said.

"Ok then," he continued, "so can you please tell me which instrument in the orchestra doubles you on this flute solo?"

Without hesitation I replied, "Yes of course, it's the bassoon."

The conductor looked at me affectionately with a smile. "Yes, that's correct," he said, "Well, I have never met a bassoonist in all my years as a conductor who could play it at that tempo! Brava!"

I was then asked to play two very difficult Strauss excerpts, which again I did cleanly and confidently, and then the audition was over. I left feeling quite good about it.

A month or so later I found out that I was given runner up. This basically meant that if the first runner up didn't take the spot, I was in. I knew how stiff the competition was, so this pleased me. Karl reassured me that this was a great result. As a sophomore in college it was good to see that I could perform reliably under such pressure. These were some of the most difficult pieces in the flute repertoire, and the experience allowed me to see that when working with a teacher who inspires and believes in you, you play your best.

The Last Flute Lesson

After four years of study with Mr. Willoughby at Oberlin Conservatory of Music, at the top of my technical game, but surprisingly with little confidence as a flutist, I returned to New York. I decided to call Mr. Bennett to see whether I could have a lesson with him again. I missed him. He was older now and living on Long Island at a beautiful farmhouse with his wife, although not fully retired. He asked me to prepare all of my orchestral excerpts for that lesson. I couldn't wait to see him again, but had not seen him for four years. I wondered what he would think of what I had become as a flutist.

In an hour's lesson, I played twenty-five of the hardest orchestral excerpts for him from Debussy, Strauss, Beethoven, Brahms, Dvorak, Ravel, Mendelssohn, Berlioz, Prokofiev, Saint-Saens and Tchaikovsky to Rossini. At the end of the lesson, he said tenderly: "My dear, you are ready." Tears filled my eyes instantly. In four years of study with Mr. Willoughby, I had never heard such support. That was the last lesson I had with Mr. Bennett.

Harold Bennett had played in a number of this country's greatest symphony orchestras under the batons of great conductors such as Eugene Ormandy and Fritz Reiner. He was also the principal flutist of The Metropolitan Opera Orchestra. He played beautifully all the way into his upper rungs with a sound that was smooth as silk. He was also able to communicate his musical ideas to his students the way a painter might, in a visual manner that really spoke to me.

He once described the opening, difficult and fast run of notes in Ravel's "Daphnis and Chloe" as "a strand of pearls. Every time I played that difficult passage of notes (an entrance that could often trip you up if you had not ironed each and every note out with equal attention) the image of a beautiful strand of precious pearls, evenly strung, helped me to play it with both accuracy and inspiration.

And although his approval that day meant the world to me, some part of me did not envision taking orchestral auditions.

Confirmations

"However many years she lived, Mary always felt that she should never forget that first morning when her garden began to grow." *The Secret Garden by* Frances Hodgson Burnett

I love this passage from my favorite children's book, The Secret Garden. I believe that my own secret garden door opened the summer of 1980 at Tanglewood, when Leonard Bernstein called me "an artist."

During those cool Berkshire summer nights in my dorm room under the eaves, beside my dear friend Willa who was carving reeds for her oboe, I quietly painted flowers at a small desk. There was no need for note perfection there.

Many years later, when selling my collections of original textile designs to various fashion houses along Seventh Avenue, one particular encounter marked yet another turning point in my life bringing vivid clarification to the choice of leaving my musical life to pursue a career in art and design.

Entering a small dress house in the fashion district, I did my usual displaying of prints upon a table for an older gentleman, whom I later learned had been a former art professor at the Parson's School of Design. Throughout this print appointment, he remained quiet, said nothing. I usually interpreted silence as a form of rejection; that the person on the other side of the table didn't like my work. At the end of the meeting, he finally broke the silence and asked softly:

"Where did you study art in school?"

With my head down, thinking he was about to say something hurtful, I replied, "I didn't go to art school. I was a music major at Oberlin Conservatory of Music."

"No wonder," he said shaking his head, "Your artwork is full of lyricism. Thank God you never went to art school! They would have destroyed that!" It was at that moment that I realized that all of my years of serious and dedicated flute study were not futile. According to this former professor at the Parson's School of Design, my love of music had found its way into my designs. My beloved stepfather Ernest wrote a poem about me back in the 1990s that my mother gave to me after his death.

Kim:

An almost free spirit,

Caught up in a world requiring conformity

And asking her to dampen her bright ideas.

No matter in which accent she stands alone with clear-eyed,

clear-hearing views of a sometimes unfathomable, ugly world,

And somehow, designs delight.

Coming out of her salad days into the spotlight.

Taking Flight

After many years of traveling around the world, from Australia, New Zealand, Tahiti, the Cook Islands, Samoa, to numerous trips to Brazil, Canada, islands in the Caribbean, Haiti, and living in Belgium and traveling around Europe, I found myself unable to board a plane.

I had actually always loved flying. I got excited by the little blue lights lining the runways; the slow acceleration to lift-off. I was not afraid of terrorism. I had spent thirty-one hours in a plane traveling from New York to LA, LA to Hawaii, Hawaii to New Zealand and finally arriving in Melbourne, Australia. I was never fearful of such lengthy trips.

But one day that all changed. When boarding a plane to go visit my brother in Louisiana, I suddenly bolted from my seat, moving a stewardess swiftly aside at the very last moment, saying in a state of panic:

"Sorry, I have to get off the plane!"

Heading quickly for the exit door that was just about to seal shut, I ran up the ramp back towards the airport gate just before the plane pulled away. Out of breath and full of sudden confusion, I ran to a payphone to call my brother, crying. I had to tell him I was not coming, which was a great disappointment to us both.

From that moment on, I would not fly for twenty years. Like a stroke victim losing the ability to speak words familiar to her all throughout her life, I was faced with a crippling impediment; one that would greatly affect my freedoms and wanderlust for many years to come.

Friends spoke enthusiastically of their travels. There were many business opportunities, award ceremonies abroad, designer collections launched both here in the U.S. as well in London that I was unable to attend as the celebrated designer. There was always a deep sense of disappointment as these beautiful life opportunities passed me by.

Throughout those years at ground level, I painted thousands of gardens both on canvas and textile designs. I learned how to travel in a different way. I found my sense of expansion in the embrace of New York City where the soil was full of rich color and life.

My first husband Marcelo, a Buddhist, once said to me in my early twenties when I was too restless to fully acknowledge his wisdom:

"Kim, *everything* is right here."

Mexican flower vendors at the Union Square farmer's market filled my arms with Dahlias for free. Tibetan boys selling apples and vegetables there greeted me with equal reception and warmth. The more I opened to where I stood, the greater my appreciation was, for *everything*. I could transport myself anywhere in the world at any moment. I was really learning how to walk.

Felipe and I circled the Central Park reservoir with our beloved dogs Maggie and Wendy for almost thirty years, through the snowdrifts of winter to the hot days of summer. Those walks, in every season, were always full of joy. Our dogs loved the park: from the deeply earthy scents of fallen leaves along the path, to the stray tennis balls hit outside of the courts that they carted home. Cherry blossoms were bursting with pink blooms around the perimeter; one special part of the park was our designated "Giverny" because it's arched apple trees reminded us of a French landscape painting.

The Metropolitan Museum of Art was our wedding anniversary ritual, accompanied by a romantic stroll through the snowy drifts of the park in winter. And every spring we went to the ballet at Lincoln Center to see Paul Taylor whose costumes in vivid colors and contemporary choreography set to great pieces of classical music and jazz had us dancing out the door.

Inside of Grace Church along Broadway we listened to the resident organist playing free Bach concerts at lunchtime. This old gothic cathedral was as magnificent as Notre Dame or any I had ever seen in France; it's high ceilings and pillars reaching towards Heaven. We found peace and a connection to the Divine in there.

Like a wave continually lapping the shoreline, and folding over itself day after day, the city continued to wash up its many treasures; from enduring friendships and colorful, urban encounters, to unwanted pieces of furniture that Felipe proudly carted home for me to paint up in floral pattern.

In 2008, when my art and design book was published, I was invited to speak at F.I.T., The Fashion Institute of Technology, to the students and faculty. The Director of the Surface Design Department, John Dowling, asked:

"Do you travel a lot? You and Felipe both to me seem like truly quintessential New Yorkers," and went on to say, "as we all know about this city, *everything* is right here."

Was the smell of freshly baked croissants in a Manhattan bakery any less enticing than a *Patisserie in* Paris? What was better about being anywhere else in the world?

Again, in Robert Frost's poem "Birches." he writes:

"Earth is the right place for love, I don't know where it is likely to go better."

The years on the ground had a lot to teach me. I was learning to walk differently. Friends were leaving the city saying impatiently, "I can't stand being in New York City during the summer," then hopping flights to Europe. They would return and still complain.

But Felipe, Wendy and I sat under trees in Washington Square Park, drinking in the local color. We found our pleasures in simple things, and in being together. Friends from abroad would come and visit, from Brazil to Slovenia. We would take them for a summer's walk along the East River boardwalk and they would tell us, "This reminds me of the Thames."

A Nod from the Universe

When one of my very talented flute colleagues at the Oberlin Conservatory of Music, tragically passed away, I was suddenly reconnected with many former musician friends and Oberlin flute colleagues I had not seen for decades.

I was eager to hear about their lives. One flute colleague Bill, who had a successful career performing in the top Broadway musicals, asked me whether we could meet for coffee. We had not seen one another for thirty-three years. He came with a letter in hand that I had written to him right after college, during my very early secretarial, corporate years in New York City.

Bill spoke honestly and candidly about his own very challenging musical journey in Manhattan after graduation, sharing that even with his impressive resume of top flute teachers endorsing his talents, and a polished command of orchestral repertoire, he was in one instance, "denied" the right to even audition for a top symphony orchestra in the country. After pressing for an audition however, (which by law he was entitled to), he had advanced impressively to the final round. He shared that three of the four judges who had heard his audition expressed that he was worthy of this position, but ultimately, they had someone else already lined-up for the post. Politics had clearly played a role in the outcome. Not wanting to live in Timbuktu playing Principal Flute, but instead living in an exciting city, he knew that he had to find his way towards meaningful musical employment and he became a highly sought after Broadway musician.

I was full of questions. We compared notes about our Oberlin Conservatory experiences and studying with Mr. Willoughby. We both loved New York City, and fought hard to find fulfilling careers here. At an outdoor table on Broadway at Union Square, our eyes locked and cheeks tightened from smiling at one another. We were both clearly happy with the career choices we had made.

Coming of Age on Seventh Avenue

Only the day before, I was invited to have dinner at a restaurant in front of Carnegie Hall with a few of my family members. I had not been to this zip code for some time. Walking past the front entrance of my third job in Manhattan after college, at the music management, I paused before the building's ultramarine blue awning on West 55th Street. I was incredulous to be standing there again decades later. It felt like many lifetimes ago that I sat behind that old typewriter that had no erase key in that dimly lit office. Memories of my early twenties instantly returned.

Walking past the facade that had once been the beloved Patelson Music Store, more musical memories resurfaced. The Carnegie Deli on 7th Avenue was now all boarded up, a landmark family restaurant where we had gathered in celebration for my brother's wedding engagement, and an after party for a dear friend's Mozart Piano Concerto performance in Carnegie Hall. The restaurant's bright yellow iconic signage was now covered with wooden boards, reminding me of a bandage over a mastectomy.

A block down on West 53rd Street and Seventh Avenue was my first music-related office job at Hi Fidelity Magazine as Associate Editor. Somehow that building more than any other along Seventh Avenue, triggered the early growing pains of my twenties. Right beside it, the Sheraton Hotel, where I had briefly attended the National Flute Convention on my lunch hour - a pivotal moment that brought up deep questioning and confusion about my decision to have walked away from my flute career.

Seventh Avenue best represented my coming of age. I felt quietly nostalgic sitting at Trattoria D'el Arte's table, seated with members of my family. The yellow cabs were whisking by the front window, against the distinct, red brick color of Carnegie Hall. My twenty-five year old nephew was seated across from me at the restaurant table.

"You were the reason, Gabriel, that I started writing my memoir," I told him. "It was your internship at the ad agency on Columbus Circle three years ago that made me realize, after seeing the excitement in your face that I once was like you."

"Aunt Kim," he said, "I know it's crazy, but I want change. I know I have a good job in New York City and I should be grateful to have it. But I just want to know how it feels to do something else, sometimes. I want to play my guitar more. Maybe I can walk dogs for a while to pay my rent? I feel like I wouldn't mind a little struggle," he said smiling.

His words could have been my own at twenty-five. My nephew was lucky to have landed a more creative type of first job right out of college. He was already using his graphic design skills to earn a decent salary. Except for his internship on Columbus Circle, it was the only job he'd ever had in New York City. I knew not to advise him one way or the other. I trusted that he too would find *his* way.

"Financial struggle is painful," I told him. "Maybe you need to feel some of that pain in order to have perspective on where you are now?"

The corporate world had caged my creative spirit too in my early twenties. Commuting an hour by subway each day from Queens into Manhattan for five years had ultimately sent me in the direction of packing my bags and running off to Europe with another man.

Always looking for the meaning and symbolism in everything, I realized that the Universe wanted me to return to this zip code so that I could have a clearer perspective on all I had journeyed on this small island of Manhattan. Despite the landmark restaurants and quaint shops gone forever, I felt happy inside.

That evening my mother and brother were going to hear a Carnegie Hall concert of a classical Romanian pianist, Radu Lupu. I had grown up listening to his piano recordings of Brahms Intermezzi and Rhapsodies. My mother, a highly accomplished concert pianist, was also a writer for a popular piano publication and had forged meaningful friendships with many of the world's great pianists after interviewing them for Clavier magazine. Making his way slowly up West 56th Street towards the green room entrance, and hugging my mother affectionately, Radu warmly greeted us all outside the side street entrance, then swiftly made his way into the hall.

Throughout my childhood, these types of encounters with great musicians were common occurrences. My parents took us often to hear the finest musicians in concert such as: Arthur Rubenstein, Isaac Stern, Leontyne Price, Jean Pierre Rampal, Luciano Pavarotti, Sherrill Milnes, James Galway, Andres Segovia, Georg Solti, to Leonard Bernstein. We went backstage afterward to meet them and get their autographs.

Decades later, (an encounter that took place thirty-five years *after* a Carnegie Hall concert I had attended with my family) in Balducci's, a former New York gourmet market on 6th Avenue in the West Village, I was standing at the deli counter, and only an inch away, clad in turban and a brightly colored wrap, was the great opera soprano Leontyne Price. It took me a few seconds to gather the confidence to say:

"Ms. Price, I just wanted to thank you a little bit late for an absolutely beautiful performance of the Verdi Requiem in 1976 with the Chicago Symphony under Solti's baton."

Leontyne Price looked at me in disbelief and said kindly:

"My dear, you don't look old enough to have been at that concert! "Smiling with a glimmer in her eyes and chin held high in true diva form, she said proudly, "I remember that performance well. I was in excellent voice then."

We both laughed and hugged affectionately, and said goodbye a few moments later.

After dinner with my family across the street from Carnegie Hall, Felipe and I drove down Seventh Avenue into the heart of busy Times Square. I usually avoided that artery because of noise and congestion. This ride felt differently. The city sparkled like a treasure chest, with bright lights flashing and bustling energies. Making our way through the fashion industry streets where I had wheeled my heavy print cases selling my textile designs to hundreds of clients, and then past 34th Street and Macy's, Felipe said triumphantly, "And whose collections are carried at Macy's, honey?"

While our car was stopped at a traffic light in front of an Art Deco doorway on Seventh Avenue and West 36th Street where I had held my very first fashion industry studio- painting job, and had been fired for not knowing how to use a ruling pen, I quietly smiled.

"Your Gardens Are Full Of Stories"

Two years into living in Stuyvesant Town, in our very green and culturally diversified city enclave, I found myself in the presence of one of the loveliest families.

On the Stuyvesant Town Facebook Page, I noticed a moving sale with a few photos of interesting pieces of furniture. I needed nothing. There was a wooden bookcase that had elegant glass doors, a pure Arts and Crafts gem. I instantly felt it would look beautiful in our home, so I enquired about the price. They were practically giving it away. When asking for their address, we discovered that we were close neighbors. They lived in the building adjacent to ours.

The following day, before heading off for my morning gym routine, I went to see the bookcase. The family members selling it were from Katmandu, Nepal. The young and beautiful wife was a graduate of Columbia University, and her husband, a recent NYU graduate. Their ten-year old son's brilliant smile was so incredibly sweet that I felt I was in the presence of a little Prince. The grandmother was wrapped in a hot pink sari, seated quietly on their living room sofa, warmly smiling.

Offered Nepalese tea, and with a hint of Indian spice in the air, we sat for an hour talking about Buddhism. I had spent twenty years working with Gil, my Buddhist healer. In my gym bag I brought along one of my wool, hand embroidered pillows that had been made by artisans in Nepal to show them. I wondered since they were practically giving away this beautiful bookcase, whether they might prefer two embroidered pillows in exchange.

When I mentioned the pillows were from my designer collection I was asked:

"What do you mean this is from your designer collection, Kim? What do you do?"

I had not spoken of my career or line of work with them. Not wanting to take up more of their time any further, I said:

"If you put my name into Google, you will see what I do."

Everyone in the room took turns holding the pillow and appreciating the beautiful craftsmanship. Soon after I thanked them for the tea and lovely visit. "I will meet you later with the fifty dollars for the bookcase. My husband will carry the unit upstairs to our apartment when it is convenient to come and pick it up. We can text each other later if that is OK." I said. A few hours later, Felipe arranged to pick up the lovely bookcase from their apartment.

We invited them to come up and see the piece in our library, where I had cleared a space for it already. Everyone agreed that it looked beautiful situated there.

"After you left our apartment, we all looked at each other like: "Who is this person that just entered our home with so much positive energy? And then I Googled you! Why didn't you tell us you were famous?" he said laughing. "I told my wife, "We should have grabbed her pillows!" We all laughed. "I have already discussed this with my wife, and we don't want money for the bookcase. We want to give it to you as a gift for the beautiful energy you brought into our home yesterday," he said. And with a smile he added, "Would it be OK though for us to keep the pillows?" (I was of course, extremely happy to give the pillows to them.)

On our bedroom wall was a hand painted wall-sized tapestry from India that had been hanging for twenty years. The painting was a depiction of Krishna amid twenty- six cows. "You know the story of Krishna don't you, Kim?" the wife asked. I had to admit that I did not. I had just been attracted to the beauty of this hand painted Indian tapestry with all of the beautiful cows looking lovingly up at Krishna.

"Krishna was a flutist like you, Kim," she said kindly.

I was speechless. I was not aware after all of those years that Lord Krishna was a flutist. In this particular tapestry, there was no flute image in his hands.

"Krishna was loved by many. All of the animals loved him, especially the cows that followed him. He was a cow herder. Wherever he went, when he played his flute, they all followed. He was so beloved," and she added, "Krishna had one love in his life, named Radha."

I took her across the room to show her another Indian painting that I had purchased at a flea market of Krishna seated beside a woman.

"Yes, that is Radha," she confirmed. "That is the love of his life. Whenever you see any painting of Krishna with a woman, it is always Radha."

In the living room they shared their visions to start a business in Nepal upon their return to their homeland.

"We wish to empower and employ poor women in our country. There is great poverty in Nepal and we want to give back. Living here in New York has been a great experience for us. We will miss living here so much in Stuyvesant Town. I cannot believe I wake up each morning to the sound of birds. We feel very fortunate to have lived here."

A few days later, after having given my design book to the family along with the pillows and a few other gifts, I was handed a pair of beautiful silver earrings from Nepal.

"I want you to have these, Kim, they are from our country."

For many years I had dreamed of running my own art school for children. I had the sudden desire to invite their ten- year old son to my dining room table to paint. I had seen one of his lovely watercolor paintings tacked on the wall in their apartment that day when visiting the bookcase that gave me the idea.

"Years from now, my son will understand what a great privilege it was to paint at your table," the mother said endearingly.

When they arrived at our door, the grandmother instantly said aloud, "Oh my God. I want to spend many hours in this home! It is so beautiful! I love flowers so much."

The dining room statement wall was papered in my orange flowers from my new wallpaper collection, and with more floral upholstered pieces on linen around the room- as well as paintings and pillows. The grandmother looked at everything with eyes wide open. But it was something she said after handing her my children's book that moved me more than anything; something no one had ever said to me before.

"I can see that your gardens are full of stories, Kim."

I hardly knew how to respond to her words. My eyes were instantly welling up with tears. She was able to see *inside* my gardens. She understood that behind the flowers were many tales.

"Yes," I said taking her hands in mine, "You are quite right. My gardens *are* full of stories. Thank you for seeing that." We didn't need to say more.

At the dining room table, while ten -year old son was painting in vivid colors that I had put out in small plastic pots, creating what looked to my eyes like an early Sonia Delaunay abstract watercolor painting, I showed him one of my art books full of Delaunay's beautiful work.

"You see here, your painting is just as good in my opinion!" He giggled with delight.

I enjoyed in particular, sharing my experience at Scholastic where the head of the children's imprint made me take my elephant illustrations out of the garden saying, "No one would understand why an elephant was standing in a garden." I figured that if anyone in the world was going to understand why elephants were standing in a garden, these new Nepalese friends would!

"It's almost like he had no imagination," the ten year -old Prince, Biraj, replied. We all laughed.

"And just to think a bookcase brought us all together," the mother sweetly added.

When in the presence of these beautiful new friends from Nepal, I felt most alive. Indeed, this beautiful bookcase in our home had "brought us together" – another story behind the flowers.

Lizzie's Visit

At one of my early fashion studio design jobs, working for a Canadian fabric converter, I met Lizzie, a talented textile artist. There were only five painters in that studio. We became good friends over the course of that year together.

Lizzie was an energetic, lovely, twenty-something year old, Korean artist. I had not seen her for thirty years. I remember how she would arrive at the art studio each morning dressed in high, black, platform shoes, short, flirty, printed cotton dresses that she sported well. Always entertaining and quirky, she made her entrance with funny excuses for her tardiness to work. Everyone adored her Bjork-like style.

Thirty years later, I received an email from her. "I was in an art supply store in San Francisco looking for something colorful. I reached for this book that was on display, and said aloud: "Oh My God! I know her!" After purchasing my art and design book, she decided to get in touch with me. A year later, she returned to New York City with her son and husband and we arranged to meet at a local cafe.

We hugged and laughed instantly, as if no time had passed between us.

"After you left the company, a few years later, Robby (another gifted Indonesian artist in the studio) told all of us, "Kim has become really big.

And we were like, "What do you mean really big?"" Robby told us about all your successes in the design industry. We were all just blown away."

Lizzie married a foreigner, had a son, moved to the West Coast for many years, and had put painting aside while raising him. In her first emails she asked me questions about my life in design, my career path, sharing that when she had stayed in a Napa Valley hotel with her family, she discovered my paintings in reproduction hanging on the walls of her hotel room.

"I keep seeing your work everywhere," she said.

She was a talented painter herself, whose technique amazed me back in the day. She told me she was still painting but referred to the service work she was currently doing as a freelance artist as "slavery." I remembered the way I had felt when designing in fashion studios in my twenties before I had decided to leave that whole 9 to 5 studio world behind. When painting became a chore, it was time to leave, I always felt.

"Why did you leave our studio back then, Kim?" she asked. "Were you unhappy there?"

"I needed to earn more money," I told her, "I wasn't sure how much longer they were going to keep me on anyway. Diane told me that the company was thinking to downsize our art studio. I figured I was going to be cut since I was not as well trained as everyone else in there. I went out and found another job right around the corner on 6th Avenue at another fabric converter. I was there only three months," I told her.

"I never changed jobs all of those years," Lizzie told me. She had remained there at the Canadian fabric converter long after I had left.

The truth was, that first art studio was a very nice place to work. All five of the artists in the room had good chemistry and a gift for gab that was lively throughout the day. We shared many of the intimate details of our personal lives with one another. Stimulating conversations were a daily accompaniment to our 9 to 5 painting hours and helped move the hours along.

Duncan, a British artist in the studio, was both a wonderful textile designer as well as a very talented fine artist. He was witty and colorful and a damn good painter. Diane, was the easy-going Canadian studio manager who basically kept us all in check, gently. She was not a tough task master type. We had many lunches together in Bryant Park on the open lawn behind the NY Public Library during the warm summer months; and during winter days, at the seedy, little coffee house across the street.

"Of all the artists I know Kim, you became the most successful," Lizzie said at the café table.

I looked across watching her gingerly eating a piece of broiled salmon on a bed of fresh vegetables. I remembered how much in awe I was of her artistic skills in my twenties, the ease with which she could knock out some of the most technically challenging painting assignments. I also remembered the delicious looking lunches she made for herself- Korean dishes of vegetables and rice.

When we left the café, I invited her to visit our apartment and meet Felipe and our sweet dog, Wendy.

"I want to see your home," she said, "I want to see your paintings in person."

In front of my "Urban Garden" painting hanging directly over the living room couch, she gazed up at it for five minutes without saying a word.

"Kim, this is just so free," she said.

Like we had always done in the studio setting in our twenties, Lizzie opened up about her life with total candor. It was when she told me that she had not flown for eighteen years that my mouth dropped open.

"Lizzie, for real?" I asked in astonishment.

"Oh My God, me either!" I told her without hesitation. She looked at me incredulously.

"You're kidding me, right? How is it possible Kim that with your success, you have not flown?"

For the next few hours, we sat in the living room sharing feelings that were extremely personal, about this similar impediment. We had both been living our lives for a long period of time at ground level. We both had embraced Buddhism. We understood the meaning of being *present* in the moment and walking. She opened her bag and handed me a book by Thich Nhat Hanh, the well-known Buddhist healer whom Gil had introduced me to, and gave me a lovely Tibetan brass bell she had brought for me. The title of the book was, "How To Walk."

Through the hot summer night in the East Village, down streets she had frequented in her twenties looking for a café that no longer existed, we were back in time, two young girls in our twenties, laughing and feeling wild.

"I am finding that all of my old friends from the East Coast have really ripened in the best way with age," she said. "They have all matured and now possess wonderful wisdom." I adored her more when she said, "I personally love growing old." I did too.

We shared our mutual interest in holistic forms of healing. I told her:

"For years when I suffered from anxiety attacks and couldn't even drive across a bridge or go through a tunnel, I learned the value of deep breathing. It took lots of practice, patience and discipline. I was so opposed to popping a pill to numb my way out of pain. I just felt it was important to *feel* it and go *through* it."

Lizzie understood. She said that friends had offered her "natural remedies" swearing that such drugs would help her and get her flying again. She never accepted them. My Buddhist healer Gil always said to me, "If the mind says no, then the drug won't work for you. It's not right for *your* particular healing process."

We sat on an old iron bench outside another café on Avenue B looking directly into each other's eyes. Her son and husband would soon be coming to get her. I congratulated her on the success of her first flight after eighteen years from San Francisco to New York.

"I feel my time for flight might be coming soon too."

"You don't need to go anywhere, Kim. New York has *everything*, let's be real," she said.

TJ

On a bench during a hot summer day in Stuyvesant Town, waiting with our beloved dog Wendy for Felipe to come home from a real estate class, an old Indonesian woman sat quietly beside me with her cane. In truth I was not in a great mood. I had hoped to sit alone in the shade undisturbed.

"How old is your dog?" the woman's soft voice asked.

Not eager to engage, I replied briefly, "She is twelve."

"I am 90 years old," she shared.

Her name was TJ. She was proud that she never required a doctor's attention since arriving in this country decades ago. She attributed her good health, she said, to holistic supplements that she took regularly, walking all the way to China Town to pick them up. She had come from a wealthy family, produced a few daughters, left it all behind to come to a country she had no work or emotional connection with, she said. What I liked about her was that she spoke of everything with great humor and levity.

"Are you the sign of Sagittarius?" I asked. I had guessed her sign correctly. She looked at least twenty years younger than her actual age; her shiny jet-black hair topped by a baseball cap.

"Call me TJ. No one can pronounce my real name correctly," she said chuckling.

"Can I buy you a cheese Danish at the farmer's market? Can we meet here tomorrow at 12:00 at this same bench?" she asked me warmly. I could not refuse her sweetness. The next day we met on the same bench while my husband was in class. She handed me a soft brown bag with two fresh cheese Danishes inside, pastries she had just gotten for both Felipe and me.

"I love to give," she said to me with a smile. "If you give, when you die, everything you have given, will come back to you."

A week or so later she phoned me at home. "I have some necklaces made of stones. Do you like stones? They have healing powers, you know. I want you to come over and choose one that you want," she said.

Aware of the healing powers of stones, I was excited by the invitation. In her very cluttered Stuyvesant Town apartment, tables stacked with all kinds of food, and bottles of herbs, she led me to a box containing about ten necklaces, some made of garnets, some of amethyst.

Amethyst was my birthstone. There were small plastic bags marked with information about each one.

"Choose one for yourself," she said. "Put that one on," she said immediately, noticing that I was looking at an amethyst necklace with interest. "Let's see how you feel in it," she said.

I walked to the mirror and held this juicy purple strand of chunky amethysts up to my neck. I usually didn't like wearing heavy necklaces. I had a lot of neck pain from years of painting thousands of textile designs in an awkward, compromised position. But I felt an instant attachment to this hefty necklace- not only because of its beautiful purple color, but because I had never had anything like it before. Something about it gave me instant confidence. It was substantial, present and generous in size. It reminded me of something one of Henri Matisse's Odalisque's would have worn.

"Are you really sure you want to give this to me TJ?" I asked.

"Yes, I am," she said, "When you get home, run the stones under cold water to remove anyone else's energies in them. Cleanse them before you put them on or hold them, say a mantra in your head. Always say that prayer before you put them on. I always say that if something speaks to you, then it's yours," she said sweetly.

I instantly thought about the day I had encountered our beloved dog Wendy on Union Square and how her eyes spoke immediately to my heart. Without hesitation I filled out an application for her adoption, and that was one of the best things I had ever done in my life.

"Are they speaking to you?" she asked.

I didn't even want to look at the other ones in the box. "Oh yes!" I said to her, hugging and thanking her. "I love these!" Although I could see through the plastic Ziploc bags that the other daintier necklaces were also very pretty, this one really spoke to me.

TJ was a devout Muslim who had a guru.

"Allah hears all my prayers, and if you need money, then pray for that," she said again.

I held the heavy amethyst necklace in my hands like ripened cherries. It was just so beautiful. I was still uncomfortable with her generosity. "I don't deserve this necklace TJ, I don't think I can accept it," I said.

She looked at me smiling. "The Universe wants you to have this. You *do* deserve it, Kim. All gifts come to you because you deserve them."

When I got home, I did as TJ had instructed, washing the stones under cold water and then putting them around my neck to "clear them of other people's energies." I was not instantly comfortable with such a generous gesture. Instead I cupped them in my hands for a while to feel their pleasing weight and shapes. I did as she had said and sent my prayers directly into them. "The key is, you have to *believe* in what you are asking for," she told me. "Don't just ask for something without meaning it. You have to know that you truly deserve it."

Here is where I started to begin realizing that TJ's message was more important than her generous gift of the amethyst necklace. Many opportunities had come and gone in my life. Many of them left me wondering "why" they appeared and then disappeared into thin air. Had I felt worthy or unworthy of them? Was there some thing that got in the way of my sense of worthiness? Felipe always said to me,

"You are very uncomfortable receiving gifts. You just like to give them."

I even remember the astrologer I had met when living in Belgium, who told me in her thick French accent when interpreting my astrological natal chart, "You love to *heeve*." (give)

I sometimes struggled with my mantras when holding the amethyst necklace and asking for help or things that I wanted. TJ told me to keep the stones cold for greatest affect. There were actually times when I felt an electric current running through my hands when holding them. Even if just momentary, little surges were powerful. I didn't doubt TJ's words. I did as she suggested, praying for a few things I dreamed of manifesting.

Manifestation: A London Launch

My favorite childhood books were all of English origin. One in particular illustrated by Maurice Sendak called "Sarah's Room" a pocket-sized book left a huge impression on me. The opening verse was:

"In Sarah's room green trees grow tall and morning glories bloom; and of all the rooms in all the world, the best is Sarah's room."

Although the illustrations were mostly in black and white of vines and flowers climbing up a child's bedroom wall, this type of lush garden interior was what I dreamed of having in my own room. I wanted my bedroom walls to be covered with Heavenly blossoms.

"The Secret Garden" was another favorite English childhood book. The central theme here again was a garden. I was drawn to its delicate floral illustrations and to the garden's interior that was eventually transformed by loving children.

I dreamed most of creating floral wallpapers and fabrics. I patiently held the vision of bringing the joy and exuberance of a garden into people's homes in this way all year round.

It would take more than ten years however, of my design life, to find the perfect wallpaper and fabric - licensing partner for our brand. We met with many UK and US companies. These meetings would typically last for hours going through hundreds of my hand painted archival designs on paper, linen and silk. It took time and careful selection because printing both fabric and wallpaper was a heavy financial commitment and investment for any company producing them.

Before digital printing, when fabric companies relied on rotary printing, fabric and wallpaper companies were not keen on working with me. Although they liked my designs and expressed enthusiasm about seeing them printed on silks and linens, my floral designs were simply painted in too many colors. With rotary printing, each color was a separate screen, therefore, a separate cost. Many of my designs had more than fifty colors. For this reason, the printing process could become very expensive if a design had too many colors.

Thankfully, years later when digital printing became popular, a simple scan of an original design could now replace the rotary screen cutting charges and printing process. All colors could now be reproduced. Every motif and every shade of green or pink, as per the original artwork, could be captured in a scan and then printed directly onto the surface of the fabric.

I have always found it difficult to paint a design using just a few colors. Painting a garden is like composing a symphony. Colors need to modulate like keys. A garden can hold harmony and dissonance visually, and chords of many sonic colors.

So after a decade of trying to find the perfect licensing partner to produce a wallpaper and fabric collection for our brand, we finally signed on with a British company, Clarke & Clarke. There was instant enthusiasm and excitement around this launch. I felt incredibly inspired to finally be creating my dream wallpapers and fabrics. Hot pink, bold and sumptuous flowers were bursting with life. My densely populated, exuberant wallpapers were influenced by the English Arts and Crafts Movement, but bolder and more modern in shape and color.

Our very first meeting with Clarke & Clarke, in our Gramercy Park brownstone living room, ran seven hours straight. I showed them literally a thousand textile designs - some new, and some from my archive. We all edited this massive assortment of designs to thirteen we would put into development. We agreed they would be printed on velvet and linen. The Art Director finally decided we should name the new collection: "Kim Parker: Art Book Collection." My first collection would be sold in decorator showrooms in ninety-two countries.

Discussions of my London launch and all of the many details were being carefully put into place. There would be a press party with magazine editors, decorators and industry buyers to be held at The Covent Garden Hotel's "Lyric Room." The launch would be a little less than a year away.

Not having flown for a long time, twenty years to be exact, I realized that I had to get myself into a plane again to get my wings. I saw this as a hugely inspiring reason for me to finally take flight again. Felipe and I booked a short flight within the US for a simple three-day vacation the following June. We booked and paid for this short trip in advance of my London launch to ensure flight to London after that, make flying again easier.

What I never could have anticipated was that our landlords of fifteen years, would tell us we had to vacate our brownstone apartment and be out of there two weeks before my London launch. We now had four and a half months to find a new apartment.

To make matters worse during that time, my beloved stepfather Ernie was hospitalized and hanging on for dear life. The stress on every level was incredible. Those six months of searching for another Manhattan apartment, (as detailed earlier), boxing and packing; a stepfather's very fragile health, a flight I knew I needed to take to dissolve fears, and an upcoming big London launch swiftly approaching, almost lead to a nervous breakdown.

It was six stressful months of exhaustion and anxiety. No one but Felipe could see the heavy emotional and physical toll it was taking on me. At the buzzer, with just a week before our brownstone lease was to expire, we finally found an apartment. We moved in quickly, but had to forego our little vacation to get our wings as it happened that same weekend we moved into our new home in Stuyvesant Town. Thankfully, my stepfather's health had improved. With just two days before me, to pull myself together for my London flight and wallpaper and fabric launch, I could not gather the courage nor energy needed to attend.

The collections were still launched in London as planned at the Decorex Show and received wonderful reviews. The Art Book collection was now featured in ninety-two showrooms worldwide, with full-page advertisements and editorial appearing in *House Beautiful, Ideal Home, Architectural Digest* and beautifully featured on the cover of *Country Homes & Interiors* magazine. UK newspapers such as: The London Times featured my floral wallpaper and wrote:

"Kim Parker's "Tatiana" new wallpaper for Clarke & Clarke nails paradise indoors."

Reflections in a Taxi

Our US fabric and wallpaper distributor held a special event at their New York designer showroom in the D&D Building to introduce my new wallpaper and fabrics collection for Clarke & Clarke.

Felipe and I grabbed a cab uptown to East 55th Street and Third Avenue to the D&D Building right across the street from Bloomingdale's. I was not sure that I would get through the event, as tragically, my loving stepfather Ernie of thirty-five years had passed away suddenly of a heart attack just a few days before. Committed to this special launch event, I knew I could not cancel. Scheduled to appear on a panel before a few hundred distinguished industry designers and decorators to introduce my new wallpaper and fabric collection, it seemed like the worst possible time for me to have to do that.

Making our way uptown in the pouring rain, passing the stock brokerage on East 53rd Street where I had worked in my twenties as receptionist, I felt emotionally drained by my entire New York journey. Although grateful to have this wonderful fabric launch and event held in my honor at this beautiful showroom, I could not shake my grief. The taxi ride felt like an endless strand of Manhattan jobs held over the course of thirty-three years. Out the window, everything was a wash of grey in the pouring rain. Pulling over in front of Bloomingdale's where my first bedding and bath collections launched in 2004, this memory seemed almost to have happened in another lifetime.

In the entrance to the showroom at the D&D Building, a beautiful sofa was newly upholstered in my "Ariadne's Dream" floral linen fabric. The moderator introduced me as "A *rock star from London*" (making reference to my designer collaborations with UK companies over the course of fifteen years.) Everyone laughed. I was nervous. On a screen to my right were projected images from my new fabric and wallpaper collections for the decorators to see. I worried that I might collapse from sheer heartbreak, but somehow I enjoyed speaking about my inspiration behind these floral patterns; the influences of painters such as Bonnard and Vuillard, the Bloomsbury Group, and the patterns of the English Arts and Crafts Movement.

Ariadne's Dream Floral Design by Kim Parker

A Magic Flute

While living in Stuyvesant Town, with no therapist landlords living directly below us anymore, I started to play my flute again more often. Not long after, I was recording Bach with a wonderful pianist in his studio and forming a chamber music group with a few string players.

On the way to a rehearsal, walking towards a beautiful, old stone church on Henry Street, on the Lower East Side and Chinatown I was finding my old musician's stride again. This particular city stretch was pleasing to me; a neighborhood that still held onto its edgy old New York charms bordered by looming, silver, newly erected buildings.

Walking by small cafes, and bodegas along Avenue A and Essex Street these small home baked businesses felt like an anachronism; a neighborhood not yet devoured by banks and generic commercial enterprises. With my new flute secured in its case underneath my arm (strapped to me the way I remember it was three decades back at Tanglewood amid the scent of pines) I reunited with my old, familiar musician's cadence. I was taking my time in a gradual crescendo towards the church to rehearse a Bach Concerto.

After decades of my design life in full force, and not performing, I felt a desire to practice Bach. A month later, while rehearsing a flute Sonata with a fine pianist whom I had just met, one of the instrument's keys was not working properly when pressed. There was no way to continue the rehearsal with the flute not functioning.

For my sixteenth birthday, my parents had given me a beautiful Haynes flute; Haynes considered one of the finest flute makers of the world. It had a warm and dark, rich sound. Throughout those early musical years, whether at Tanglewood under Leonard Bernstein's baton, or all throughout my flute study at Oberlin, the Haynes was the flute I performed on, only twice needing an overhaul.

Feeling slightly exasperated that my faithful Haynes was now not playing properly and needed repair I entertained purchasing another instrument. Not wanting an interruption to my rehearsing schedule while it was in the repair shop, I went on Ebay to look at used flutes. After some searching, I came across a Japanese model, a Yamaha. A fellow Oberlin Conservatory flute colleague, Bill, had once highly recommended this maker as "a good back- up instrument." Japanese flutes were known for having a brighter sound.

When committing to the purchase of this Yamaha flute, I agreed to meet its former owner, a lovely, young twenty-something year old girl, at The New York Public Library. Sitting outside on one of the old stone benches that late summer's day, I superficially ran scales up and down the instrument, attempting to quickly familiarize myself with its action, before handing her the cash. It seemed to play with relative ease.

What I could not have anticipated, was that this new Yamaha flute would open a magical door to The Secret Garden. I quickly discovered that everything I had ever wished to musically express through my silver flute, was flowing effortlessly. I felt like Pan. Its sound was resonant and clear. Every note seemed to rejoice. Six years prior, when visiting my New York psychic Louise in Hell's Kitchen, she said firmly, "Kim, *sound* wants to return."

But there was more to this Divine exchange in front of The New York Public Library that revealed itself to me thirty years later. In my hometown of Huntington, LI in 1989, when performing at a public library, with my mother at the keyboard, something traumatic occurred in my musical life. It was perhaps the single performance that really put a stop to my flute career.

If all things are *Divinely aligned* (as I believe they are) then that difficult and painful performance was perhaps part of the Divine Plan. An old friend and oboist at Oberlin (who had also shared a room with me at Tanglewood) said to me after that 1989 library performance, "What happened to you, Kim? The only piece in the concert that sounded like you, was the solo piece."

Thirty-three years later, before the majestic façade of The New York Public Library on 42nd Street and Fifth Avenue, a young, brunette girl in a floral dress who reminded me of a younger version of myself in my twenties, soon rushing with just an hour's time back to her desk in a midtown corporate setting, handed me *my song*. It took me a few days before I was able to see the symbolism of the "library" and this magical full circle.

But as the morning fog lifted quietly along Avenue A walking towards Henry Street to rehearse a Bach Concerto with Sam, my violist, in the Santa Teresa church, I stopped in front of the local flower displays to smell the freshly cut bouquets of roses. Peeking in the window of a yoga center, an old sign in Hebrew hanging faithfully from a fire escape above, the city and I were in perfect harmony.

Vuillard House

There is a beautiful painting in pale pinks of a dog sleeping on a bed that now hangs directly over our pink sofa in our Brooklyn living room. The artist is Mary Abrams. She and my mother were friends throughout my childhood; two highly exalted aesthetes who shared a mutual love of printed fabrics, Bonnard, Vuillard and eclecticism.

As a child, when first entering Mary's house (many years before her son William and I became romantically involved), I felt as if I was entering an actual Vuillard painting. Her three-story colonial was a museum. The pink velvet Victorian sofa, hassocks covered in patterned fabrics, throws strewn over armchairs, and best of all, Mary's oil paintings on every wall - composed a living Vuillard painting. Her dachshund was usually curled up on some velvet chair - a la Bonnard, in a room dimly lit by vintage glass lamps. These early childhood visits with my mother to the Vuillard house, never seemed long enough for my young eyes. I remember the early sense of awe her work inspired. I didn't know back then that my future would eventually be that of a painter too.

By the time I was sixteen, her son William and I were serious high school "sweethearts", (although somehow that term "sweethearts" would not adequately describe the intense and passionate relationship we shared.) Our early romance was more like the one in "Sophie's Choice," between Kevin Kline and Meryl Streep; a complex love affair at a young age. Three entire decades after William had tragically passed away, and while his father and I were putting together an art book manuscript of Mary's paintings to present to my editor at Harry N. Abrams, he shared:

"You know Kim, you were the love of William's life."

These words were delivered decades later, and held great meaning for me. I was just twenty something when my mother called me to tell me the tragic news. Although happily married to my first husband at that time, it was a quake to the heart.

Many years later, while happily married to Felipe, the two of us visited Mary at her Long Island house. I had just started painting on silk, and I very much wanted to share my portfolio of hand painted silk designs with her. I really respected her artistic opinion. Mary took many of them in her hands with the same appreciation I held for her paintings. After complimenting one particular floral design in my collection, I handed it to her as a gift. I was touched, a few years later when seeing it framed on the wall in her bright white art studio. Years later, when I was giving my late beloved grandmother Grace, a small garden painting for her 90th birthday, my grandmother declined the gift, saying politely, that she didn't really understand it. Grace responded to more traditional paintings and less colorful artwork. Mary, however, who happened to be there in the room that day, stood up and said emphatically, "'I'll take it!" - words that meant so much to me. Mary also had a set of my floral Spode dessert plates that she told me she loved using.

During the time while working on Mary's art book manuscript submission to Abrams, in appreciation for the work I was doing, she bestowed a small original painting of hers upon me: a gorgeous depiction of white wicker chairs on her screened porch. It is a painting that I use often when teaching adults and children- that illustrates her brilliant economy and use of white.

When Mary sadly passed away a few years later, I went to sit shiva at the Vuillard house. It had been some time since I had seen William's older brother, and been inside the house. I entered this enchanted interior yet again, with the same feeling of awe I had as a child. Nothing in that regard had changed. Mary's paintings were all still hanging on every wall, and his older brother kindly encouraged me to "take a walk throughout the house to see all of her work."

A few years later, when the father sadly passed away, it really felt like the end of an era. I knew that the Vuillard house would be up for sale in my hometown not long after. I spoke with William's brother at that time, and conveyed how the three paintings I had acquired from his mother held such inspiration to me and also inspired my young art students. "Why don't you come over before I sell the house," he said kindly, "walk through it, and select whatever paintings you want."

I will start by saying that this day might qualify as one of the best days of my entire life. Felipe and I walked slowly hand in hand the way couples do in a museum, through the many hallways and into the many rooms of this gorgeous colonial house. We were both speechless. There were just too many beautiful paintings to take in. The selection process felt almost impossible. There were gorgeous landscapes, interiors, gardens, beach scenes, portraits, dog paintings, and still lives large to small. As judiciously as possible, I put a few aside the ones that were speaking to me. One only has to imagine being told to go into a museum and choose a painting you always wanted to possess. That is what it felt like.

Years back, I had remembered a painting hanging in the hallway that haunted me of their dog. I combed the house and found it, still quite taken with its beauty. But another dog painting was calling me. The one I thought I had wanted, I didn't choose. Instead, a dog lying on a bed in a pink room, won my affection. Our living room in Brooklyn was pink. Mary and I shared a mutual love for that color.

Felipe and I went all the way to the third floor attic which was filled with more, beautiful, dusty canvases, still more possibilities. It was there that I found a rather large sized portrait of a woman seated in a chair, painted in a cooler palette of grey and cool blues punctuated by red.

"Take them both," were words I could hardly process.

This incredible moment in my artistic life, inside the Vuillard house, somehow felt like the perfect epilogue to a very long and intense novel. Soon this grand and elegant three-story colonial house of treasures and memories, the place that all throughout my childhood held great artistic inspiration, early romance, and heartbreak, delivered a profound gift. And fittingly, like the sleeping dog in Mary's soft pink painting, it could all be finally, put to bed.

Bernstein at Greenwood Cemetery

The day Leonard Bernstein died in 1990, the Earth shook for me. When the hearse drove over the elegant Brooklyn Bridge towards Greenwood cemetery, I could barely watch this procession on television, hardly believing that this Titan of the music world, and the world in general, was being laid to rest. Fans waved their handkerchiefs in mournful respect, from his Manhattan Upper West Side Dakota residence, to along the bridge itself.

It is hard to be human at moments like these, when a great Being has "departed" having left behind such an enormous mark and contribution to this Earth in such a brief time.

As early as I can remember, tucked away in my childhood bedroom, with photos of my musical hero tacked to my bulletin board, and orchestral recordings that had me leaping around with excitement behind my closed door;; like a slow and gradual meditation, I'd held Leonard Bernstein as the highest form of Divine, creative expression humanly attainable.

When at age sixteen, as a member of the youth orchestra at Tanglewood that summer, told that I would be playing one of Bernstein's new compositions under his baton, I was lifted into another realm. One thing

I seemed to know, before even playing for him, was that a great gift was being given to me.

I had never played this particular orchestral work of his before. The Boston Symphony Orchestra had premiered the composition the previous night, so there was no time to familiarize myself with the flute part. And as Bernstein lifted his graceful arms that morning, asking my name, and then saying we would begin the rehearsal with the flute solo midway through the piece, it was one of those magical moments, when life sweeps you off of your feet, with the same kind of levity of a goat in a Chagall painting. At that moment, it was just the two of us in this Divine dance, like that scene in West Side Story when Maria meets Tony and everyone around them goes out of focus. And the next thing I knew, the words, "Kim, you are an artist," were spoken, like a baptism, as he parted his way through the string section to kiss me.

That dance has accompanied my every creative endeavor; unlocking my "right" to fully embrace and express my truest feelings whether expressed in a note or upon a white surface. Bernstein never held back. He gave his soul and spirit generously in every moment, in every word, and in life. I cannot relate to anyone's criticism of his passionate outpouring. What else are we here on Earth for, if not to live life passionately?

So when Felipe and I left our thirty-three year life in Gramercy Park, Manhattan, crossing over an illuminated Brooklyn Bridge one night towards our new home in Cobble Hill, we raised our arms, just as Bernstein might have done, in sheer and utter joy. I knew that once settled, I would finally go to Greenwood cemetery, to pay respects to my beloved hero, Leonard Bernstein.

It took time to locate his resting place. Greenwood cemetery was vast, with well- groomed gardens full of flowers, birds, peace and beauty in the heart of Brooklyn. I expected to find a huge tombstone in his honor, but instead, a rather humble sized stone flatly resting on the ground beside his beloved wife, Felicia, and a bench with his name inscribed amid the embrace of shrubbery. The moment I saw his name etched in stone, I could not speak. I fell almost operatically to my knees, crying. And just in the way I had freely performed his music at sixteen, I eulogized with the same depth of feeling and ease, more than forty years ago. Placing a stone upon his grave, as is a loving and respectful tradition in the Jewish religion in lieu of placing flowers, and gently putting my right hand over his name, I thanked him. What I realized, at that moment, was that this visit brought everything full circle. I left the gravesite with a feeling of deep release, and eternal gratitude.

About the Author

Kim Parker is an internationally acclaimed and award winning lifestyle designer and artist. She is the author of two critically acclaimed books, *Kim Parker Home: A Life in Design* (Harry N. Abrams); and *Counting in the Garden* (Scholastic). Winner of three prestigious British design awards for her iconic Mums & Asters designer rug, her timeless, signature style of modern floral Art and Design has been sold worldwide at premier retailers such as Bloomingdale's, Macy's, Harrods and Lane Crawford. Since the launch of her namesake brand in 2001, Kim Parker has collaborated with top licensing partners such as Spode, Mikasa, Clarke & Clarke, The Rug Company, CHF Industries and Galison creating bestselling collections of wallpaper, fabric, tabletop, designer rugs, bedding, bath, pillows, giftware and wall art.

Visit her website at www.kimparker.tv

Follow her on social media @kimparkerstyle

Join Kim Parker Studio on Facebook, her Children's Art gallery featuring the works of her young and gifted Art students.

Kim in New York City 2022

Printed in Great Britain
by Amazon